THE THEORY OF MORALS

AN INTRODUCTION TO ETHICAL PHILOSOPHY

BY

E. F. CARRITT

Fellow of University College, Oxford
University Lecturer in Philosophy
Late Temporary Professor of Philosophy
in the University of Michigan

ἐγὼ δὲ τὰ μακρὰ ταῦτα ἀδύνατος
PLATO, *Prot.* 335 C

OXFORD UNIVERSITY PRESS
LONDON : HUMPHREY MILFORD

Mr. A. J. Jenkinson of Brasenose College read these proofs for me with the generosity and scholarly care which were familiar to his friends. He returned me the proofs on April 10 : on April 19 he was killed while climbing on Glyder Fach in North Wales.

E. F. C.

May 1928.

THE THEORY OF MORALS

OXFORD UNIVERSITY PRESS
AMEN HOUSE, E.C. 4
LONDON EDINBURGH GLASGOW
LEIPZIG NEW YORK TORONTO
MELBOURNE CAPETOWN BOMBAY
CALCUTTA MADRAS SHANGHAI
HUMPHREY MILFORD
PUBLISHER TO THE
UNIVERSITY

Corrected Impression of 1930
First edition, 1928
Printed in Great Britain

CONTENTS

ANALYSIS OF CONTENTS

WITH REFERENCES TO BOOKS

NOTE.—A name which would appear frequently among the references to contemporaries given below is that of Professor H. A. Prichard, if only his book upon the subject were ready. I owe to him as my tutor an early interest in moral philosophy, and as a friend the stimulus of frequent discussion and the patient criticism of this book in its earlier stages. As, however, he assures me that 'we seem to differ in almost every particular', I am encouraged to think that my publication may be some slight additional incentive to his own.

I. Introductory. (1) Moral philosophy arises from a natural impulse. (2) This book will endeavour to follow the development of a man's first crude theories under progressive criticism. (3) Moral philosophy begins with practical problems and the effort to discredit obligation. [Plato, *Republic*, i.]

II. Hedonism. (4) At first, attempts are made to reinforce the questioned duties by the authority of (*a*) law, (*b*) religion, (5) (*c*) general consent. None of these external standards of action are satisfactory. [Locke, *Essay on the Human Understanding*, I. iii.]

(6) The first internal standard suggested is prudence: acts which secure the agent's happiness are right. This theory is rhetorically commended on the ground that private happiness leads to public happiness; that prudence is not easy; and that many moral maxims opposed to it are superstitious. (7) This is an obviously false description of what we mean by duties. The theory owes its plausibility to a confusion of several possible meanings. (8) (*a*) That the agent's happiness follows right action, or action thought right, though he does it for a different reason. No evidence of this can be discovered empirically. (9) (*b*) That to provide our own greatest happiness is always right (Hedonism). But can there be a *duty* to seek happiness rather than anything else? Does this describe the duties that we recognize? (10) (*c*) That a man must always act from the desire for his own greatest pleasure (Psychological Hedonism). This denies any duty or moral rightness. [Bentham, *Principles of Morals and Legislation*, i; Paley, *Moral and Political Philosophy*; Moore, *Principia Ethica*, iii.]

(11) This last form of the theory is rhetorically commended on the ground that the successful pursuit of private happiness demands rare qualities. (12) Some followers of this doctrine allow that

men *have come to* act from other motives than the sole original desire for happiness by association of ideas; this contains two false assumptions. (13) And attempts have been made to support this amendment from theories of evolution. But if our belief in duty is discredited by its origin, so is science. (14) The origin of the delusion that we have duties is ascribed to a convention or contract. [Plato, *Republic*, i; Hobbes, *Leviathan*, ch. xiii–xxi.]

(15) The popularity of psychological hedonism chiefly rests on its inconsistent connexion with the doctrine that we 'should' aim at the greatest happiness of others (Utilitarianism). This connexion rests on two confusions. (16) (i) That the greatest pleasure of the greatest number always seems to me to be (*a*) either the same thing as my greatest pleasure, (17) (*b*) or (since that is obviously not true) a means to it. This also is only saved from palpable falseness by the argument (ii) that the pleasure of our neighbours gives us a pleasure higher in kind, though not greater in quantity, than any other. This is inconsistent with the theory. [Plato, *Gorgias*; J. S. Mill, *Utilitarianism*.]

(18) Psychological hedonism surreptitiously uses the words 'ought' and 'right' in a non-moral sense. (19) Arguments in refutation of hedonism. (20) (i) Appeal to common sense. (21) (ii) Hedonism renders unmeaning all terms of moral praise or blame and denies any freedom of choice. (22) (iii) It fails to account for either imprudence or moral struggle. (23) (iv) It makes capital out of the happiness of a good conscience; but this assumes an act that has been done from a motive other than the desire of pleasure. There are other desires more common. (24) (v) Difficulty of calculating quantities of pleasure. [Rashdall, *The Theory of Good and Evil*, II. i; Mackenzie, *Manual of Ethics*, pp. 229–232; Bentham, *Principles*, iv.]

(25) (vi) Not only do we desire other things besides pleasure, but a life in which all other motives were subdued to the desire for a maximum of pleasure is not one that most men would choose. [Plato, *Philebus*; Bradley, *Ethical Studies*, iii.]

(26) (vii) Perhaps what hedonists really mean is not that men always do what they think will bring them most happiness, but that they always do what at the time they desire most to do. (27) Some who hold this add that we have come to think some acts right and desire to do them because we originally did them as means to something else which we desired. (28) Our belief in duty can be neither disproved nor proved. Most self-evident truths are incapable of proof. For the whole of this chapter cf. Moore, *Principia Ethica*, iii; Rashdall, *Theory of Good and Evil*, I. ii; Butler, *Preface* and *Sermon I*.

III. Evolutionary Ethics. (29) Granting that we have duties philosophers have gone on to ask what they are. In this they have often confused the intellectual search for a definition of our duties with the moral inquiry what those duties are. The first problem presupposes some answer to the second. (30) A naïve answer is—Follow Nature. This is obscure. (31) It is given some meaning when nature is taken to mean evolution. But the struggle for existence only secures existence. [H. Spencer, *Data of Ethics*, ii; L. Stephen, *Science of Ethics*, ii, iii; Huxley, *Evolution and Ethics*.]

(32) Since mere promotion of life is no duty for us, some say that we ought to promote the greater power or efficiency of our species. The doctrine of the superman only introduces fresh confusions. [Plato, *Gorgias*; Nietzsche; Russell, *Philosophical Essays*, pp. 14, 15.]

IV. Utilitarianism. (33) If our duty be to promote some good kind of life for men, it is suggested that we ought to promote their happiness. (34) To hold that this is our only duty is inconsistent with a belief in justice (i) if that mean equality. [Sidgwick, *Methods of Ethics*, III. v, IV. iii. 4.]

(35) (ii) If justice mean in proportion to desert, this is defended by utilitarians as (*a*) not disappointing expectation; but this implies *just* expectation. (36) Or (*b*) encouraging useful conduct; but this either (i) tells us to pay debts when it is not useful because it generally is useful or (ii) makes justice depend upon publicity. [Mill, *Utilitarianism*, ch. v.]

(37) Utilitarianism neglects particular obligations. (38) The truth it contains is that all rational action must be meant to secure the satisfaction of some one. (39) And that therefore the consequences of action must be considered. But all the consequences, not only pleasure, and also the antecedents must be considered. (40) Utilitarians have often inconsistently allowed that pleasures differ in quality as well as in quantity. [Mill, *Utilitarianism*, ii.]

(41) Since men have other motives for acting than the desire of pleasure, we may have other duties to them than to give them the greatest pleasure. And it is urged that if *we* should be moral but only make *others* happy our 'good' would be different from theirs. [J. Grote, *Examination of the Utilitarian Philosophy*.]

V. Perfectionism. (42) Does our duty, then, consist in making other people good? (43) This maxim is criticized as being (i) vague, (ii) impossible, and (iii) useless. (44) (i) The precept of making men good is hardly vaguer than that of making them happy. [J. Grote, *Treatise on the Moral Ideals*, xiii.]

(45) (ii) It is impossible to make men *good* in the sense of (*a*) moral or meritorious. But in the senses of (*b*) doing right acts or of (*c*) having virtuous inclinations, it is possible. (46) (iii) This criticism rests on the assumption that the value of right action is in resulting happiness, which perfectionists would deny. [T. H. Green, *Political Obligation*, A.]

VI. Self-sacrifice and Self-realization. (47) Sacrifice of anything is always for the sake of realizing something else. My desires inconsistent with realizing my idea of what is right ought to be sacrificed. (48) If self-realization does not mean selfishness it seems to mean doing what we think right. [Bradley, *Ethical Studies*, vii.]

(49) The self which I ought to realize is not the self which I know and which acts, but an 'ideal' self, myself as I ought to be. [Croce, *Pratica*, II. ii, 2; Gentile, *Logica*, Parte IV, cap. viii.]

(50) There is no peculiarly insoluble contradiction between self-realization and self-sacrifice. [Taylor, *Problem of Conduct*, iv.]

(51) Acts thought right are thought of as in some measure satisfying somebody, and the doing of them in some measure satisfies the agent. But the acts which produce the greatest satisfaction are not always thought right, and the agent's moral satisfaction depends on the act being done because thought right. [J. Grote, *Treatise on the Moral Ideals*, vi.]

(52) The analysis of the right act into means and end, or intention and consequence, is a misleading abstraction. The value of a whole need not be the sum of the values of the parts. [Moore, *Principia Ethica*, § 18; Laird, *A Study in Moral Theory*, pp. 43–8.]

VII. The Common Good. (53) The doctrine that right conduct consists in the pursuit of the common good is an attempt to escape these abstractions. Its meaning is obscure. [T. H. Green, *Prolegomena to Ethics*.]

(54) The term Common Good is ambiguous. It may mean either a common source of satisfaction or (55) an act commonly thought right. [Rashdall, *The Theory of Good and Evil*, ii, p. 96.]

(56) It is not always our duty to produce the first or to do the second. (57) A later form of this view holds that all goodness is created by willing, and willing is good in proportion as it is *coherent* with a deliberate policy (*a*) of the agent, (*b*) of others. [H. J. Paton, *The Good Will*.]

(58) This depends upon (*a*) an ambiguity in the term *good*, (*b*) the assumption that right or coherent action is the deliberate policy of all men, (59) (*c*) the circular argument that right action is action which coheres with right actions. (60) It also involves the dilemma that either coherence, though good, is not created by

willing or, if it be, then anything willed as good is good. (61) The theory is rendered plausible by some elements of truth.

VIII. Right and Good. (62) The acceptance of a true moral philosophy need not involve any improvement in the conduct of those who adopt it. (63) The aim of moral philosophy is theoretical. But false philosophies are apt to distort practice. The cure is a true philosophy. [Bradley, *Ethical Studies*, v, pp. 174–6.]

(64) Most moralists have tried to deduce the rightness of acts from the good which they tend to bring about. This is impossible. [Prichard, *Does Moral Philosophy rest on a Mistake?—Mind*, 1912; Rashdall, *The Theory of Good and Evil*, i, pp. 135–8, 188–94, 240, 266–9; Russell, *Philosophical Essays*, p. 31 (and cf. pp. 4–7); Moore, *Ethics*.]

(65) The *Summum Bonum*. [Aristotle, *Ethics*, I. i–iv; Kant, *Critique of Practical Reason*, ii. 2.]

IX. Duty for Duty's Sake. (66) Can the rightness of particular acts be proved from the idea of duty? [Kant, *Foundation of Metaphysics of Morals*, i.]

(67) Kant attempted to give an affirmative answer to this question. But he failed to distinguish right from moral acts and he tried to prove the rightness of acts without consideration of consequences. [Rashdall, *The Theory of Good and Evil*, I. v.]

(68) His test of self-contradiction does not pretend to suggest right acts. It is not even successful in detecting wrong ones without consideration of consequences. (69) He is driven to supplement this negative test by a consideration of consequences in his maxim that we should treat moral beings as ends. This is ambiguous. (70) So far as Kant tries to pass beyond a formal analysis of duty his doctrine is unacceptable. [Bradley, *Ethical Studies*, iv.]

(71) The supremacy of the moral judgement does not exclude but rather presupposes the presence of desires.

X. Idiopsychological Ethics. (72) This is the name given by Martineau to his theory, implying that it is, in Kant's sense, truly 'critical'. (73) The salient data of morality are praise and blame, self-approval and remorse. These are said to depend on the worth of the motive or spring of action. [Brentano, *Origin of the Knowledge of Right and Wrong* (English translation), pp. 9–25; Martineau, *Types of Ethical Theory*, vol. ii, and vol. i, Introduction.]

(74) But the worth of an impulse depends upon the object to which on any particular occasion it is directed; that is, on the rightness of now gratifying it. [Sidgwick, *Methods of Ethics*, III. xii.]

(75) My duty is to try to do what is absolutely right. I may

succeed in doing what is right for any one who is in my situation of partial ignorance. [Russell, *Philosophical Essays*, pp. 22–5.]

XI. Rights. (76) Utilitarianism and Kant's formalism alike, in common with all systems so far discussed, fail to emphasize particular obligations. We commonly speak of rights, but our meaning is obscure. (77) Since legal rights are not the only rights we hear also of natural rights. But it is objected that rights depend upon 'society'. [Green, *Political Obligation.*]

(78) And, further, upon a society that recognizes a 'common good'. Against the obvious interpretation of this view the theory of natural rights protests. But it cannot distinguish natural from other rights. [Ritchie, *Natural Rights*, i, ii, v; Moore, *Principia Ethica*, § 28; Bosanquet, *Philosophical Theory of the State*, viii.]

(79) Rights and duties are said to be correlative. Are there any acts right for me to do which are not my duty and to which nobody has a right? (80) A suggested differentia, that men have only a right to be let alone and that this is my only *duty* to them though it may be *right* to help them, is unacceptable. (81) Those who deny the validity of the distinction allege that it is based merely on the expediency of enforcement. [Rashdall, *The Theory of Good and Evil*, I. viii.]

(82) But against this it can be urged that it is often right to waive one's rights. (83) The best solution seems to be that duties which other people have a right I should do are right acts that are very obligatory. (84) Rights only seem absolute and duties only seem generically different from other right acts when they are stated generally in the form of laws.

XII. Punishment. (85) The merely utilitarian or exemplary account of punishment is inadequate as taking no account of guilt. [Rashdall, *Theory of Good and Evil*, I. ix.]

(86) Even the reformatory view of punishment is by itself inadequate to describe the essence of punishment. The essence of reward is not educational nor exemplary. Punishment and reward imply desert. [Bradley, *Ethical Studies*, i.]

(87) Forgiveness, too, would be inexplicable on utilitarian grounds, but remorse involves remission of retribution. (88) Retribution is not vengeance nor the *lex talionis*. Punishment is the expression of condemnation, which incidentally must give pain as remorse does. It is right to feel remorse or, failing that, to be given punishment. (89) There is no need for a general scale of equivalence between guilt and pain. [Rashdall, *Theory of Good and Evil*, i. 289.]

XIII. Moral Rules. (90) No rules obviate intuition: (*a*) whether this is an instance of the rule, (*b*) which of two conflicting rules is here paramount. What validity rules have is first seen in instances, from which rules are then derived. [Laird, *A Study in Moral Theory*, pp. 78–9.]

(91) Rules do not help us to know what is right, but may save us from doing what is wrong. (92) Rules and resolutions made in advance are irrational or only rational in the sense of useful concessions to our own irrationality. [Croce, *Pratica*, Parte III.]

XIV. The Moral Faculty and the Moral Motive. (93) The word 'faculty' is dangerous. (94) What are the resemblances and differences between the moral activity, exclusive of the act of choice, and (*a*) reason and (*b*) desire? (95) To judge an act right is not very similar to desiring to do it even after reflection. [Plato, *Republic*, 436–9.]

(96) The recognition of the rightness of an act is a sufficient ground for choosing to do it as against a desire to do something else. [Hume, *Principles of Morals*, App. I.]

XV. Freedom. (97) Actions are distinct from events. Any mechanistic view which denies the distinction is untenable. [Lotze, *Practical Philosophy* (Ladd), iii; Spinoza, *Ethics*, III. 2.]

(98) Self-determinism holds that our acts spring of necessity from our own nature or character and are therefore free. [Green, *Prolegomena to Ethics*, II. i.]

(99) Kant's evasion of the difficulty by his distinction of phenomenon and noumenon is unsatisfactory. [Kant, *Foundation of Metaphysic of Morals*, iii.]

(100) Does the theory that our acts spring necessarily from the nature of our self account for a freedom which would justify remorse, censure, and punishment? [Russell, *Philosophical Essays*, pp. 30–40.]

(101) Freedom of choice seems demanded by morality and only by morality. [Bradley, *Ethical Studies*, i.]

(102) Theological objections have been raised to freedom of choice. But the alternatives between which I choose being determined and my belief as to their consequences being fallible the ultimate result of my free choice might be knowable. (103) The problem of freedom is closely related to the problem of evil. [Descartes, *Meditations*, IV.]

XVI. Conclusion. (104) A justification of the terminology arrived at. (105) A summary of the chief positions maintained.

I
INTRODUCTORY

(1) Of all the questions raised by philosophy those about duty are, I think, the most natural to ordinary men. It is easy to live, and even to live an intellectual life, without ever asking what truth is or how we come to know it; and only the born metaphysician is apt unstimulated to observe that behind the results, and behind even the ideals of science, there lurks a problem as to the ultimate nature of reality.

But there is no man who has not been confronted with a duty which he would rather leave undone, and this weakness of the flesh is a more usual beginning than pure wonder for moral philosophy. Once the critical faculty has been turned upon the idea of duty, it is only moral or intellectual sloth that can avoid the whole process of ethics. For, I suppose, it has never been seriously questioned that conduct can be judged; that in action, as in thinking, there is a better and a worse way. Whatever it may turn out to be, and for whatever reason it may be so, we must all agree that one of the kinds of behaviour possible on any occasion is better than others. And even were anybody so fond of paradox as to deny this, it would be incumbent upon him to explain the growth of the universal delusion that it is so; to do which, he must examine the various forms which the delusion has taken; so that for him, no less than for the rest of the world, a theory of morality will have its interest.

(2) Since problems about the nature of duty were the most pressing in philosophy, they seem to have been

the first that were clearly separated from poetry and from science and studied by themselves. And I doubt whether in any branch of philosophy progress so easily appreciable has been made. Nowhere, at least, have the confusions and ambiguities of early thought been so much cleared, and the fundamental problems made so definite and so intelligible.

For both these reasons then, because the question is one in which every man has an interest and because the answers are answers that will interest him, I believe moral philosophy to be the best approach to philosophy. In that belief, I have tried to write an introduction to the subject as simply as I can, seeking to avoid technical language, and hoping rather to stimulate the reading of more adequate books than to presuppose it. Under the summary of each section in the table of contents I have referred to books which state and criticize the view I am discussing.

The same belief has guided me in the choice of my method. Since it seems to me almost incredible that any of my readers can have failed already to ask themselves what may be the validity and the nature of their duties, and probably to have given themselves some answer, I shall try to follow what I take to be the natural development of the normal reflective mind. What that natural development is I can judge partly by the recollection of myself, partly by that of the many pupils from whom I have learned. Being the normal individual development, it will naturally not vary greatly from the order of the various schools that have arisen. But these have, in the history of philosophy, sometimes occurred out of what may be called their natural sequence, through the idiosyncrasy of some great thinker. In particular, the clearest and most persuasive formulation of some relatively naïve view may have occurred quite late in the history of thought, when perhaps it had in fact been already decisively refuted. I shall therefore follow the 'natural' and not the historical order of theories, beginning with the simplest or crudest; showing how this fails to satisfy and is criticized and replaced by another, which itself in turn suffers the same fate. My method will be dialectical rather than dogmatic, endeavouring to work from what is more popular to what is more true.

The drawbacks of such a method are obvious. There must be much repetition. It will often seem that the same question is asked again and again in only slightly more precise terms, and answered with only slightly greater conclusiveness. In the beginning we can hardly avoid a rhetorical way of talking, which can but gradually approximate to precision. For many of the most popular theories owe all their plausibility to loose statement.

In spite of this, I think it is the best method. For, as Plato said, philosophy is not a thing which can be put ready-made into the mind; God forbid! Its value lies as much in understanding the wrongness of the wrong answers as in knowing the right; indeed the latter is impossible without the former. In science we may perhaps fully comprehend the Copernican astronomy without having appreciated the Ptolemaic, but in philosophy the individual reproduces the errors of the race, and he who has not strayed with the heretics is here but unstably orthodox upon hearsay. The only way of converting any one to a philosophic view is to show him that it necessarily grows out of reflection upon what he already believes. I have therefore flattered myself that, following the path which I have planned, I might pick up some of my readers at various stations by the way to take them some stages with me, and hoped that those who have already traversed the earlier part of the journey will have patience till I overtake them.

(3) This insistence of moral questionings in life is naturally mirrored in every branch of literature. No one can read such plays as the *Antigone* or *Measure for Measure*, such historical commentary as Macaulay's Essay on *Clive* or the *Melian Dialogue* in Thucydides, such novels as *Les Misérables* or *The Brothers Karamazov*, not to mention more didactic works like *Marius the Epicurean*, without asking himself several of the questions which will concern us. For such questions arise out of life itself. We say that it is wrong to lie. But surely there are cases where it is permissible and even obligatory to say what is not true. My questioner may not have the right to a truthful answer. Whether in this particular case he have the right, I alone must judge; for no general rules can ever exactly fit a peculiar case; and did they never so nicely, it is only I who of my own conviction can accept them. What then is the nature and authority of duty? What are our duties? What makes a right?

II

HEDONISM

(4) Doubtless in very early stages of reflection it was sufficient to appeal to some external authority, such as law or custom. But state law or family custom only supports our beliefs about our duties while no support is needed; the prop and the fabric are apt to decay together; one of the first duties to be doubted is the duty of obeying some law. Historically, moral scepticism arose with the discovery that different states had very different laws.

So behind the mutable and arbitrary codes was sought the law of God, of which they might be but corrupt interpretations. But a code claiming religious sanction was no better. Men soon learnt that here too there were other claimants, by no means always agreeing with their own. Divine laws, like all others, demanded interpretation before they could be certainly applied to particular cases; and, moreover, once men were inclined to criticize them, could easily be shown to be of doubtful authenticity, corrupted by tradition, obscure, metaphorical, and misunderstood.

It is simply not conceivable that the most recondite criticism of texts, the most conclusive study of evidence, the most metaphysical theology, should establish the divine authority and the validity of any precept deliberately repudiated by our conscience, such as to stone the sabbath-breaker; or even of anything obviously indifferent, such as to abstain from things strangled.

The only justification of any code is its claim upon

our moral consciousness, in fact, the recognition that it needs no justification; and that is just what the critic whom we are considering will not allow. If he is not sure that some particular precept has the validity it claims, then to refer him to the code which contains it merely drives him to question the validity of the whole code. The only way for religion to convince his conscience would be to show him that the situation in which he has to act or the result of his action is not what he supposed. And he may suspect he has mistaken situations in which an authority that usually commends itself to his conscience contradicts it. It is our own conscience which first gives the authority weight, and to which it must finally appeal.

(5) The suggested authority of a universal consensus of mankind is even less satisfactory. Such consent would be a more plausible guide than the tribe, but unfortunately it cannot easily be found. Infanticide, slavery, and other customs now condemned were approved or suffered by the highly civilized Greeks; as are suttee, polygamy, and suicide by some modern races. To eat your parents, to sacrifice your firstborn, to refrain from washing; there is hardly anything so monstrous or so trivial that it has not been considered somewhere a duty, though somewhere else a crime. For one man private property is the sacred foundation of society, for another it is the source of all injustice. Plato, the puritan and the greatest of philosophers, advocated the abolition of marriage. Whether you count or weigh the authorities you will not escape dispute. And so men are apt to doubt if the duties most accepted to-day are anything but the prejudices of convention and training. It is not easy to be uninfluenced by surroundings and

tradition. Had we been born in another continent we might not have inherited from chivalry an ideal of honour, but might have shuddered at the pollution of our caste or the impiety of taking animal life. The northerner is apt to condemn passion, the southerner to despise calculation. Take no thought for the morrow, give to every one that asketh, turn the cheek to the smiter: what is the relation of these maxims to the duties of thrift, of philanthropy, of respect for law?

For the interpretation of every maxim, and that really means for the choice of his maxim on each occasion, the inquirer is sent back disappointed to himself. He must bear his own burden. But all these considerations are superficial. The fundamental difficulty is that, even if we believe universal consent to be approached more and more nearly on some highly general rules—as that kindness is better than malice or truthfulness than falsehood—yet the man who is inclined to question them will not be greatly moved by the fact that others are not. Indeed it is the glory of the few individually great moral reformers in history that they have doubted the idols of the race and stood alone against the world; as it is the tragedy of every inconsiderate 'idealist' to find that in fact he was not wiser than the ages. The agreement of other men, especially of enlightened and good men, with my moral judgement is a provisional testimony to its truth, just as it is for my theoretical judgement; for neither can it be more.

(6) In default, then, of any external standard, is there nothing, we may ask, in the nature of acts themselves which makes some right, some wrong? Perhaps the most obvious attempt at an answer is that, at all events, actions which injure the doer are foolish and therefore

wrong, and those which benefit him are right. I can understand the common voice which bids me not to be intemperate, dirty, spendthrift, or idle. Ordinary prudence forbids me to endanger my health or livelihood, openly to break the law, or even to make myself unpopular. And, if it generally pay to keep the law, it always pays to render ostentatious and scrupulous homage both to law and to promise-keeping and all such ties of honour; for thus I shall encourage others to honourable conduct, which in the long run will be for my advantage. If I happen to set a high value on the more refined pleasures of ambition, of art and intellect, of the emotions, and of society, I shall further see the wisdom of a good deal of laborious self-improvement, self-restraint, self-denial, and discrimination. Moreover, since I am naturally not without affection and sympathy, I shall, if I wish for a happy life, duly indulge these propensities and behave with generosity to those who attract me or to refuse whom pains me; my relatives and friends, perhaps the poor or my country, will be sources of gratification to me, at least negatively, since they are occasions for indulging deeply rooted impulses, which it may be easier to relieve than to forget. So far indeed is this theory from desiring to appear the champion either of gross profligacy or of heartless prudence that it often poses as our saviour from the superstitions and pharisaism under which the world has groaned. *Tantum religio potuit suadere malorum*[1] is its pious lament over the persecutions, hardly more cruel than the asceticism of the martyred, the rejection of beauty, of love, of genius, the multiplication of burdens practised by puritans in every age. It

[1] Lucretius i. 101.

points at the vindictiveness of a Tertullian or a Dante, the self-torture of a Simeon Stylites, the hypocrisy of a Tartuffe, the ugly narrowness of fire-and-brimstone reformers. It claims to be on the side of the elect and gentle humanists, Aristippus with his urbanity and the genial charity of Montaigne and Shakespeare:—'Because thou art virtuous, shall there be no more cakes and ale?' —and St. Francis himself, to whom all the world was brother. Was it not the hedonist Aristippus who said, 'It is more pleasant to give than to receive', and Epicurus who counselled the happy man to die for his friends? Even God loveth a cheerful giver. To his fellows the sight of a happy man would be no common pleasure. And the man who seeks happiness wisely is long-suffering, reasonable, a shunner of violence, no busybody, temperate, a seeker of beauty and intellectual goods; a better citizen and a more comfortable friend and master than the intransigent Stoic whose pride peeps through the holes in his garment. It is the canting moralist who sours both himself and others.

Such is the rhetoric of the cause. We must presently sift its grain of truth from the chaff in a more prosaic style. And first we must warn ourselves against judging a theory by its immediate fruits in the conduct of those who hold it. It has been grafted with human nature and, for a time at least, bears fruit which is not its own:

Miraturque novas frondes et non sua poma.[1]

(7) It is true that most of the daily 'duties' recognized by an average respectable citizen, and some of a rarer kind, may seem to be covered by such a theory as this. It is arguable that it *covers* many of the right acts we do,

[1] Virgil, *Georgic* ii. 82.

but does it give any account of what we mean when we call them duties? Though right acts are often beneficial in the long run to the agent, oftener perhaps than he can foresee, this is not the reason he thinks them right, any more than their immediate unpleasantness is, though they are often unpleasant. Perhaps if we all really lived a life of enlightened and consistently selfish prudence, we should be not less, maybe more, useful wheels of the social machine than we are; but we should not be acting from a sense of duty to others. We should behave more industriously, more civilly, and more temperately than we do, and so doing we should do rightly, but not because it was right. Though there would be fewer unpopular reformers, martyrs, and champions of the oppressed, there would be no drunkards, idlers, spendthrifts, or gamblers. Though there were less devoted love and friendship there would be no crimes of passion or revenge.

And so to some it has seemed a simple and obvious truth that right conduct is that which will lead to the agent's greatest happiness, and moral conduct is that which he thinks will do so. But the simple answers of common sense, like those of other oracles, owe their plausibility to a doubtful meaning.

(8) (*a*) One meaning, though an unnatural one, might be that if you do right or try to, it will, in ways that you cannot foresee, turn out to be for your greatest happiness. This is a metaphysical or theological assertion about the nature of the universe which does not concern moral philosophy and which I have no wish to question. The Psalmist who had never seen a righteous man begging his bread may have thought it true even of this life. The Psalmist who observed the wicked

flourishing like green bay-trees may have required another world to redress the balance of this. But both must have meant by righteousness something different from mere prudence, if they thought it something which *deserved* reward. They acknowledged a duty which was not the same thing as seeking pleasures, though they thought that all these would be added to it.

(9) (*b*) Secondly, this answer might mean, and strictly should mean, that those actions and only those are right which will as a fact bring us in the end the greatest happiness, and that consequently morality consists in doing what we think will bring us the greatest happiness. This is the doctrine called Hedonism. But to this many plain men would reply that it seems false. For the phrase 'I ought', if it has any meaning at all different from 'I want', implies 'Whether I want or not'. And it seems, to the plain man at least, absurd to tell him that he ought to try to get the greatest pleasure whether he want it or not. He might admit that he ought to try to get his own greatest happiness rather than the second pint of beer which at the moment he desires more. But he may happen at the moment to desire the welfare of his country or of his children, or the advancement of knowledge, or the leaving of an unsullied reputation, more than he desires what appears to him likely to lead to his happiness upon the whole; and it will be hard to convince him that patriotic or parental or scientific effort, or even the pursuit of posthumous fame, is wrong. And he often thinks he ought to sacrifice the happiness he does want.

In other words, the contention that a man *ought* always to effect his own happiness is so absurd that it would hardly have been maintained had it not been confused with a third possible interpretation of our oracle.

(10) (*c*) Those who hold that right conduct is that which achieves the agent's greatest happiness have usually implied that the only motive from which men can act is the desire for their greatest happiness. This is the psychological doctrine called psychological hedonism, which leads to our third interpretation. On this view every man does what he thinks will lead to his greatest happiness, and consequently it is impossible to make any distinction of morality or desert among men. By luck or wisdom some of them perhaps may do acts which in fact will lead to their greatest happiness, and these might perhaps be called by the psychological hedonist right acts. But if so, the word right could only be used in the sense of 'suitable for bringing about a certain end' as it is used in such idioms as 'you are going the right way to get yourself into trouble'. In this sense of right there is no more meaning of duty or obligation than in the phrase 'a right line'. There is a similar ambiguity in the word 'ought'. 'You ought to keep your word' implies obligation unconditioned by any desire of the agent. 'A tyrant ought to be ruthless' implies that ruthlessness is necessary to success as a tyrant; here there is no more meaning of obligation than when we say, 'You ought not to have such a quick pulse'. Similarly also the word 'good' sometimes means efficient. In this sense 'a good man' means 'a man good for any post' because capable of achieving almost anything he wants to. But such a man, if he wanted to do something wrong, would turn out, as Plato saw,[1] a very bad man in the moral sense.

[1] *Republic* 334.

If all acts are done from the desire of happiness, we can only distinguish some of them as right in proportion as they secure it. So long as hedonism admits that we desire other things besides a maximum of pleasure, assuming we can choose which of our desires we will satisfy, there is sense in asking which we ought to satisfy. If it replies, as it does, that we ought always to satisfy the desire for the greatest pleasure, the only objection is that we none of us feel any *obligation* to do so. But a theory which asserts that we *cannot help* doing what we think will bring us most pleasure has precluded itself from asking or answering any question about what we *ought* to do. It can only discuss the wisdom of our forecast. For it virtue is knowledge. It may say that action which *does* secure the greatest pleasure is 'right', but by 'right' it can only mean 'guided by a correct calculation of results'. And since it is bound to assume that every one *must* do his utmost to calculate results correctly it cannot say that we *ought* to calculate them correctly. The former kind of hedonism misdescribes our moral judgements, the latter denies that we make any. I suppose psychological hedonists could reply—though I do not remember one who has done so—that a man might recognize something which he calls a right act, though he did not think that it would lead to his greatest happiness and therefore could not do it. Just as he might know what knowledge or art is but not think either would give him pleasure. Such a man might then call people good who happen to think that those acts which they or he believe right will lead to their greatest happiness, and who consequently do them. Of course, for psychological hedonism, thinking an act right could not arouse a desire to do it, for nothing could be desired except happiness. I cannot myself find any meaning in calling an act right except that we ought to do it, or any meaning in saying we ought to do an act unless we can do it.

(11) This is a doctrine which has been so widely held, and which so constantly recurs on a certain level of thought, that we must do every justice to the element of plausibility that it contains. What, it may be asked, could a man do but that which it pleases him most to do? One man's meat is another's poison; one finds his greatest pleasure in art, another in athletics, some in speculation, some in drink, and others in charity. Some indeed mistake themselves and weary of their choice when it is perhaps too late. Something they have lost then appears to them more desirable than what they have gained; but one and all, martyrs and voluptuaries, men of business and artists, do what they think will bring them most pleasure, the pleasures of heaven or a good conscience, of sympathy, of power, of beauty, or of their bellies. What other object could they have? The 'best' are the wisest, those who are most careful not to squander themselves on the trivial gratifications of gross and deadening appetite but, realizing that the failure or success of life is at stake, discriminate and refine their satisfactions, preferring those which are permanent as well as keen and which cultivate instead of deadening the further sensibilities of the spirit. For this end most men will be wise not by any means to neglect the social relations. In the pleasures of friendship, of family life, of benevolent activity they will find sources of happiness less mixed and dangerous than in violent ambition, the gusts of selfish passion, or the solitary triumphs of avarice. But, on the other hand,

they will be very careful of accepting any conventional code of conduct. Since it is his own happiness that each necessarily tries to realize, with just his own capacities for enjoyment, he will be wise to take no man's estimate of it upon trust. So the enlightened sage sits tranquilly aloof from the prejudices of the vulgar herd, observing with pity or amusement on what strange roads they seek their happiness and how far they miss the goal. And in all the human spectacle nothing will seem to him more curious than the growth, by unconscious association or conscious fraud, of the phantom called the moral law. That which superstition once threatened with the punishment of the gods is still shunned when the gods have vanished ; what is feared and punished by the community is dishonourable even when secrecy is secure.

(12) Most supporters of psychological hedonism now add to its plausibility by impairing its consistency; they admit that to-day men have—what its earlier supporters held impossible—other motives than the desire of pleasure. But they maintain that this was not always so. By an association of ideas things originally chosen for the sake of pleasure, or otherwise closely associated with it, have become desired for their own sake. Thus the miser may come really to love money for itself, and the prudent man giving or sobriety. So a kind of act, say a just act, which men now 'think right', and may do because they 'think it right', is in fact one that they have come to *desire* to do for its own sake, though they originally did it as a means to happiness, which was all they then desired. And as the process by which this has come about is now explained to be purely irrational, the man who thinks an act right—if that does not mean

thinking it will bring him most happiness—is under the same kind of delusion as the miser. In fact on this view the miser, being a man who by association of ideas has come to desire something other than happiness for its own sake, is actuated by a sense of duty. The doctrine amounts to this : once upon a time psychological hedonism was true, men only desired the greatest pleasure; owing to our tendency to refute psychological hedonism by transferring a desire to an associated object, it has become untrue; but now that the history of this change is revealed, we may lose these desires for other things besides pleasure (if we are convinced that we shall get more pleasure by doing so), and then psychological hedonism will live happily ever after. Pure psychological hedonism taught that it is a delusion to suppose that men ever do anything except what they think will bring them most pleasure. The amended doctrine we are considering teaches that men do other things under a delusion.

There are here two false assumptions. The first is that nothing but pleasure was originally desired. It is not true that we now desire sleep—as we do, even when wakefulness would be prudent—merely through an association of the ideas of sleep and pleasure. The second is that to think an act right is the same thing as to desire to do it.

(13) The doctrine of psychological hedonism is commonly supposed to have gained greatly in force by the adoption of the evolutionary hypothesis. The popular applications of this to morality are so vague and diverse that it is difficult to give them any one form for criticism.

I have not succeeded in discovering among them any additional arguments for psychological hedonism itself.

If the modification of that doctrine described in the last section be adopted, it may be urged that in the vast lapse of evolutionary time what now seems the choice of things for their own sake may have grown out of the use of them as means to pleasure. Besides the two false assumptions just noticed this further assumes the inheritance of acquired associations, which is at least doubtful. It will, however, be fair to set out the more general argument as I understand it.

By accidental variations there arose families to whose members certain types of conduct now called right, say parental self-sacrifice or mutual loyalty, were natural. On the principle of honour among thieves, these societies flourished, crushing out less serviceably prejudiced rivals: such conduct proved the best policy, and best policies survive. Here again it is not explained why loyalty is called a duty, even when unattractive, while sexual indulgence is not. I should not be surprised if it were true that the reason why we have some impulses which it is usually right and others which it is often wrong to satisfy is that the existence of both kinds is generally good, or at least not fatal, for the survival of our species. Just so I am prepared to believe that our interest in pure science is developed from a desire for useful knowledge which had a survival value. But if this humble origin be thought to discredit the moral distinctions we now make, and of which we believe we see the reasonableness, it must equally discredit all our scientific thinking, including that complex train of argument which leads us to believe in evolution. We should thus be landed in the complete scepticism of the materialist, which confounds itself; it cannot even question rationally, since for it no answer would have any truth or meaning. We must either stop thinking or return to the necessary faith of reason in itself.

Before Darwin's day we knew that the baby is not moral and is not rational; if that does not discredit our reason or our morals, no more does the fact that our ancestors were not.

(14) But long before the jargon of biology was imported into popular ethics, supporters of psychological hedonism had hit upon a device for reconciling their paradox with the apparent facts of consciousness. It is clear that acts called honest or just are sometimes performed which do not very obviously lead to the agent's greatest happiness. It had to be explained how he at least comes to think that they do. The old account of how this has happened ran as follows.

Men found it inconvenient to live in mutual violence and robbery and agreed to make laws, to punish law-breakers, and to preach 'honesty' and 'continence'. In course of time they succeeded in imposing upon themselves, and came to think that each really had an *obligation* to keep such a bargain, even when his breach of it could not be detected or punished. But if when they made the 'contract' an obligation was recognized to keep it, whether it paid or not, then there was already another motive for action besides desire for happiness. If no such obligation were recognized then anybody who keeps the 'compact' when it does not pay him is suffering from a delusion of which, if he be still rational, he will cure himself so soon as he recognizes its nature. Law and order are established and I find them useful; so I shall naturally try to enforce them upon others; but my own little violations of them will not bring them in ruins about my head while I live. True, society avenges itself upon some actions, but there are many which it cannot detect and more which it does not punish, though they are very harmful to itself and very advantageous to the doer. It would be an historical absurdity to suppose that any such contract was ever made, but many people have supposed that the moral relations of mankind are just such as would have resulted if it had been. This is a moral absurdity. For it is meaningless to speak of a 'contract' which there is no 'obligation' to keep (except the impossibility of profitably breaking it!). The obligation to keep contracts cannot be a clause in the first contract; nor can an obligation to keep them when this does not pay arise by lapse of time out of the fact that when it pays it pays. I am not here concerned with a doctrine sometimes held that all other obligations are deducible from an original obligation to keep contracts, but only with the contention of psychological hedonists that, on the supposition of a Social Contract, all obligations are deducible from self-interest. This reduces duty to a convention.

(15) Our general criticism of psychological hedonism may be briefer than our statement of it, since the arguments are well-worn and the plausibility of the theory depended on a natural confusion of thought which it was proper to present sympathetically. Few probably, in face of the obvious criticisms already cited, would have identified right conduct with the attainment of pleasure had they not made one or both of two confusions which have led to the amazing paradox that psychological hedonism was consistent with, and indeed the basis of, utilitarianism; they have identified

the pleasure of the agent with the pleasure of others, and they have allowed that some kinds of pleasure were better than the rest. These two confusions must now be considered.

(16) (1) To argue that, since desire of pleasure is the only motive, pleasure should be sought impartially for all men is like arguing that since I care for nothing but eating I should stint myself to feed the poor, or that I should turn the other cheek to the smiter because I feel nothing but anger. No other man's pleasure can be mine, though of course it may sometimes lead to it; as turning the other cheek might encourage our enemy to expose a more vital part, or as feeding my slaves might in the end feed me. The transition from my own pleasure to that of others is slurred over by the utilitarian maxim that 'every one is to count for one', which, under the innocent guise of arithmetic, introduces another ground for action besides pleasure, namely, justice. Or else the transition from my own pleasure to that of others is explicitly defended by the argument that as each desires his own happiness they all desire the happiness of all. But, since pleasure is often competitive, we might as well say that both of two antagonists desire the victory of both, which might be supposed a drawn battle.

(17) (2) Whoever then say that pleasure or happiness is the sole end must mean the agent's pleasure or happiness. When they see this, in order to keep in some kind of touch with the facts they are supposed to be describing, they hastily add that, sympathetically constituted as we are, other people's happiness may often be the best means to our own. And, passing to the second confusion, they even assert that this will

always be the fact, so manifestly are the pleasures of sympathy superior to the rest.

Now if superior meant merely greater in amount, this would be obviously questionable. The pleasures of sympathy are often dearly bought by their inseparable pains. For our own health or success we can take some measures, but to set our heart on that of others is indeed to give pledges to fortune. To narrow our sensibilities as far as possible is probably the safer policy, and in this way much may be done.

But those who use this argument have often expressly stated that by *superior* or *higher* they indicate a difference not of degree but of kind. And, for those who maintain that pleasure alone is in any sense 'good', to distinguish some pleasures as bad is a manifest absurdity. 'Superior pleasure' either means greater quantity of pleasure or it implies some quality other than pleasantness as the standard of selection. To say that the only possible motive is desire for pleasure, but that superior pleasures are or should be (and therefore can be) chosen instead of greater ones, is no better than to say, 'I care for nothing but money, but it must be honestly come by'. The only consistent hedonist is one who seeks pleasures solely according to their quantity, giving them preference as they are strong, unmixed with pain, permanent, and favourable to future pleasure; acknowledging that the objects which afford them are irrelevant.

(18) As we said before, what plausibility there is in hedonism and in psychological hedonism depends upon their confusion with one another, though they are in fact incompatible. When we are told that we *ought* to make others happy because happiness is our own *sole*

end, we can never tell in which of two possible senses the term 'sole end', and consequently the term 'ought', are meant to be taken.

(*a*) 'Sole end' may mean that whose desire is our only possible motive. If that is so, then to tell us that we 'ought' to make others happy means that this is always the correct way to get what all men must try to get, namely, their own happiness. Here duty, morality, and desert have disappeared. But nobody believes it.

(*b*) 'Sole end' may improperly be taken to mean the one thing which it is right to bring about. If it were true that our own happiness is the one thing that we ought to achieve, and also that the one way to bring this about is by making others happy, then it would follow that we *ought* to do this in a moral sense. But nobody believes that either of these suppositions is true. These two interpretations (*a*) and (*b*) then are incompatible, but neither is plausible unless confused with the other.[1]

(19) We now have the hedonistic psychology consistently before us, and we have only to ask if it truly describes the facts of consciousness. It says that no man can possibly do any action unless it seem to him productive of the greatest amount of pleasant feeling to himself. The rightness, goodness, nobility of this pleasure, not being themselves quantities of pleasure, cannot affect his choice.

To begin with, this very dogmatic and sweeping statement is strongly opposed to the ordinary view which distinguishes duty from pleasure, and the burden of proof rests with it. For it makes the universal assertion that all men always desire and choose pleasure

[1] For the two senses of *ought* cf. § 10.

and nothing else, while its opponents may be content with the particular contradiction that some men sometimes desire or choose other things. Even those who hold the ethical doctrine called hedonism—that we *ought* to seek our own happiness—are bound to deny this psychological theory; for they obviously imply that we *can* seek other things.

(20) I myself find even the most popular criticisms conclusive. Did the tortured conspirator who, rather than betray her friends, bit off her tongue and spat it in the tyrant's face calculate that thus she would obtain the greatest amount of pleasant feeling? Or did those who for the sake of love or hate have chosen what they believed a certain and eternal damnation? Or does the fairly enlightened drunkard? Or does any man who sacrifices his life or happiness in doing his duty?

(21) If we answer Yes to these questions, we should expunge from our dictionary all terms of moral praise or blame. If nobody has any choice but to pursue the single object which seems to him most pleasant to himself, praise and blame are absurd. We can only pity failure or admire skill in the involuntary chase. Each man's every action is as irrevocably fixed as the fall of a stone. Meanness, heroism, indignation, struggle, remorse are, at best, silly fables. The world is a less dramatic scene than we supposed.

(22) A little reflection seems to show that not all, but only some, actions are decided by the quantity of the expected resulting pleasure. We are sometimes speaking the truth when we say, 'I can't bring myself to do it yet (for instance, go to bed) though I know that I must do it in the end, that I shall not be comfortable till I have done it, and that the longer I put it off the less pleasant

will be my present situation (since the fire is sinking), the harder the task (since my energy will be less), and the less pleasant the result (for I shall get to bed cold);' or again when we say, 'I will do the right thing though I would rather not'. Imprudent action and moral action alike disprove psychological hedonism.

(23) It is true that in moral action, having done what I think right, I shall have the satisfaction of what is called a good conscience, but I should not get this if it had been my aim. We might as well expect to go to heaven in reward for being very much afraid of hell. We only approve ourselves, or others, for choosing duty before pleasure, or at least for doing our duty for its own sake. We could not approve ourselves for trying to do right unless our belief in the rightness of the act had been our reason for doing it. And this is only a case of the more general truth that the possibility of satisfying a desire for pleasure depends on our having other motives; for instance, desires for other things or a sense of duty. We may reflect on our particular propensities and propose to seek the satisfaction of as many as possible (that is, the greatest amount of pleasure), but if we did not instinctively desire sleep, food, exercise, power, admiration, and sympathy, then self-love (or the desire for our greatest happiness upon the whole) would have no way of gratifying itself. As things are, we may indeed stimulate a renewal of these desires by remembering the pleasure of satisfying them in the past, but we may also yield to them when we know well that the balance of pleasure is on the other side.

Indeed, the war may be carried into the enemy country by pointing out that the frame of mind when we desire nothing but pleasure is exceptional and apt to fail of satisfaction. It is usually a morbid state, occurring when we are ill or tired and our ordinary interests, ambitions, and appetites fail us. Like fretful children who ask, 'What shall I do?' we seek something to arouse us, that is, something for which we can stimulate a desire. If we cannot succeed in this, if we can desire nothing but pleasure, like the child, we had better go to bed. When he was old and ill, Horace Walpole wrote, 'I seek amusements to amuse me. I used to rush into them because I had an impulse and wished for what I sought.'

(24) Further it is at least doubtful whether the calculation of the comparative quantity of different pleasures can be carried out as hedonism requires. No doubt two glasses of beer may give more pleasure for the time than one. It may also be possible to know whether you *want* to drink the second glass more than you want to enjoy your afternoon's walk; but whether this pleasure of the palate or that of animation be greater may be as difficult to decide as whether there is more colour in blue or red. Certainly your desire for one pleasant thing is not assuaged by getting more of another. There is not a certain amount of the same indistinguishable stuff called pleasure attached to two different acts, as you might get the same shilling by work or theft. The pleasure of work is not commensurate with the pleasure of smell.

(25) Finally, even if a man could train himself to subdue all other motives to a desire for a maximum of pleasure it may be questioned whether he would choose to do so. Plato has, I think, shown that most men would not. For pleasure in the abstract—when we refuse to consider its sources—is without standard or

limit. So long as we act from no other motives (acting from which might of course bring us pleasure) than the desire for our own pleasant feeling, even in satiety we are never satisfied, since that is an appetite which grows with what it feeds on and indeed with what it sickens on. It sets the Danaid task of drawing water in a sieve. There are few pains of the mind worse than the thought of past pleasures irrecoverable.

> That a sorrow's crown of sorrow is remembering happier things,[1]

but an honest act, a scientific discovery, the creation of a beautiful thing, though they may have been on the whole painful, are in a sense joys for ever. The self-frustration which would result from trying to live as psychological hedonism supposes we all always live is well described by Carlyle:

'Will the whole Finance Ministers and Upholsterers and Confectioners of modern Europe undertake, in joint-stock company, to make one Shoeblack HAPPY? They cannot accomplish it, above an hour or two; for the Shoeblack also has a Soul, quite other than his Stomach; and would require, if you consider it, for his permanent satisfaction and saturation, simply this allotment, no more, and no less: *God's infinite universe altogether to himself*, therein to enjoy infinitely, and fill every wish as fast as it rose. . . . Try him with half of a Universe, of an Omnipotence, he sets to quarrelling with the proprietor of the other half, and declares himself the most maltreated of men.—Always there is a

[1] Ed ella a me: 'Nessun maggior dolore,
Che ricordarsi del tempo felice
Nella miseria: e ciò sa il tuo dottore.'
Dante, *Inf.* v. 121.

black spot in our sunshine: it is even, as I said, the *Shadow of Ourselves*.'[1]

(26) Psychological hedonism in fact involves a denial of all distinctions in moral worth (as well as between right and wrong) since it denies any difference in the motives from which men act. Had it avoided the blunder of supposing all desires to be desires of pleasure simply, it might have fallen back on the balder statement that every man always does what at the moment he most desires to do. And it would be almost as difficult for this theory as for psychological hedonism to retain the notion of right actions in the sense of actions which we ought to do, for there is no meaning in talking of what we ought to do if there is only one thing we can do.

I suppose it might be said that we can distinguish a right act, and if we happen to desire to do it more than anything else, whether because it is right or for any other reason, we necessarily do it, but if we desire anything else more we necessarily do that. We might then call those men 'good' who desire to do what is right because it is right (not, I imagine, if they desire to do it for any other reason) more than they desire anything else, just as we call those studious who desire most to study. We shall have to return to this difficulty later.[2]

(27) Many, though not all, of those who hold that we always do what we most desire (feeling the difficulty, which I hold fatal to that view, of finding a meaning for 'duty' on their theory) have tried to explain the belief that an act is right by the association of ideas. So far as I understand their argument, it is as follows: Some acts, such as stealing, are usually punished, and we desire to escape punishment, others are rewarded, and

[1] *Sartor Resartus*, II. ix. [2] §§ 96, 100.

we desire reward. By associating the thought of an act with the thought of its usual consequences we transfer our desire from the latter to the former, and come to desire not to steal even when detection is impossible; and desires founded on such associations have a peculiar flavour which we call thinking the act wrong or right, as the case may be. So the miser's love of money would be a moral judgement that he ought to amass it.

(28) All attempts to disprove the reality of moral obligation, to show that it is an illusory notion to which nothing or only something very different really corresponds, fail. But it may be said that all attempts to prove its reality are equally futile. And this is true. You can no more prove that there are duties than that there are beautiful things or true judgements. The truth of some judgements and the existence of some duties are self-evident. And nothing is more certain than what is self-evident, for that does not need or gain by proof and is generally incapable of it. Everything that can be proved is proved from something which is itself evident, ultimately from something self-evident, and by arguments whose validity is self-evident and cannot be proved. If everything had to be proved nothing could be, for the process would be infinite, and infinite in two directions, an infinite regress of premises to be proved and an infinite regress of proofs to be validated. The distinction of right and wrong can no more be deduced from any non-moral conception than that between truth and falsehood from anything non-rational. We see the necessity of both with equal clearness. To fail of making either would be an equally sure mark of insanity, of falling outside the human pale.

If any one ask us, 'Why ought I to do these acts you call my duty?' the only answer is, 'Because they *are* your *duty*', and if he does not see this we cannot make him, unless by informing him about matters of fact; if he sees they are duties, he can no more ask why he ought to do them than why he should believe what is true. To answer, 'Because they are the best policy', would not answer the question why he *ought* to do them.

III

EVOLUTIONARY ETHICS

(29) ONCE it be granted, then, that we have duties and that the obligation to do something consists neither in liking to do it nor in liking its consequences, whether these be natural or ordained by human or divine laws, it may seem consequent to ask what the nature of our duties is. The greater part of ethical writing has been occupied with attempts to answer this question, or, in other words, to define right conduct.

But those who have attempted this task have not always made it very clear what they were trying to do, and have, in fact, often confused two different aims. The more justifiable was to find in all the acts we think right some other common quality which makes us think them so. Such an attempted definition can be refuted if we discover that we think some acts right which do not contain this quality or some wrong which do. But moralists, in a natural desire to rebut these refutations, have often unconsciously passed to dictating what we *ought* to think right. If our moral judgements commonly refute their definition they imply that these judgements are mistaken. The assumption is that general definitions of right conduct are more certainly recognized to be true than particular judgements of what we ought to do. But, in fact, our very certainty that we have a duty depends on our recognition of particular duties, is indeed a generalization of it. To suppose that we find ourselves in the position of knowing that we have duties, but of having no idea what any of them are till the philosophers come to our aid, is absurd. A suggested general principle of conduct can only be commended to us by showing that in particular instances we do think it ought to be followed, and it can consequently be criticized by showing that we do not.

Against what has just been said it may be urged that moral judgements are often the results of prejudice and ignorance which reflection and criticism can remove. People with a moral repugnance for divorce may change their votes on consideration of the great unhappiness inflicted by its refusal in any circumstances. Those who begin by thinking it wrong for the uncongenial to live together may come to condemn facilities for separation when they consider the effect upon children. We shall have to discuss later in what sense particular moral judgements—that this act is right—can be argued. At present it will be enough to say that in the conversions just cited one particular moral judgement is substituted for another when new facts are emphasized. Certainly not all our beliefs about right conduct are equally clear and certain, and we do sometimes know that we have a duty—as to make the best use of our talents or to decide equitably in a complicated dispute—without being sure how to carry that duty out. But particular judgements about the right act in some particular situation, real or imaginary, are our only data for defining right acts. The best we can hope is that, should we discover a common quality in all our known duties, it might give a clue in more doubtful situations.

(30) One of the earliest definitions of duty was the maxim—Follow Nature. Nothing could have been less clear. In one sense everything that is must be natural or it could not exist. Or if nature be opposed to monstrosity and abortion as that which *should* be, the maxim

only bids us do as we should do. 'For nature is made better by no mean, but nature makes that mean.' But sometimes nature is opposed to the work of man—which in this sphere would be law and 'convention', —not as a higher reason than his, but as something simpler and more primitive.

> I think I could turn and live with animals, they are so placid and self-contain'd,
> I stand and look at them long and long.
> They do not sweat and whine about their condition,
> They do not lie awake in the dark and weep for their sins,
> They do not make me sick discussing their duty to God.[1]

That is a very natural mood and as proper for a poet to express as its opposite which follows in the same stanza; but when it is turned into a philosophy of life it forfeits the poet's charter of liberty: 'Do I contradict myself? Very well, then I contradict myself.' On the same counsel by which we should copy the careless birds, they should copy those reptiles who leave their eggs to be hatched by the sun. If the animals are above us because they do not look before and after, then higher still are the stones which neither seek food nor chew the cud, and the eternal strength and freshness of gravitation should point us the path of least resistance.[2]

(31) It is from the teachings of biological evolution that this maxim has first acquired some plausible meaning. Natural selection, by securing the survival of those types in a species who are fittest to survive, favours the survival of the species. And here, it has been held, we have a principle which 'at last puts morals on a scientific basis'.

[1] Walt Whitman, *Song of Myself*, xxxii.

[2] Wordsworth, *Ode to Duty*. Contrast M. Arnold, *Morality*.

First we must remind ourselves that the past history of our species does not prove that we *ought* to seek the survival of the species, or anything else, rather than the satisfaction of our own desires. We saw that the attempts to base obligation upon survival values could only lead us to think it a delusion. What we now have to consider is the different view which, granting that we have duties, suggests that a sure guide to them will be found in the impulses that survive because their possession favoured survival. And the suggestion has a pious air of enlisting us on the side of the world's process to co-operate willingly with the power that in any case rules our destiny, and to submit our private interests to the welfare of the human family. An obvious criticism will be that this really tells us nothing. Any desire which we may feel is one that is not so fatal to our race as to have been stamped out. And when I feel promptings both of pity and of cruelty it would be my duty, if I should follow nature, to follow the stronger, which is what I should have done without any idea of duty.

Probably such a principle would not have attained its popularity but for its unconscious identification of the survival of the fittest with progress. The race of men exists, and we may be right in thinking it something 'higher' than the race of earth-worms, but of a *necessary* progress, as distinct from adaptation to environment, science knows nothing. Adaptation is often by degeneration. 'The fittest to survive may be fit for nothing else.' Sensitiveness to light may be a danger rather than a safety to creatures who can manage to live in darkness. Sympathy with individual suffering would be a cause of weakness to the community of bees or ants. With changed environment the free speculation, the aesthetic faculties, the humanitarian emotions, which have hitherto been at least consistent with survival, might become distractions or positive hindrances in the tasks of nutrition and propagation. Earth-worms have existed longer than men, and if our only aim should be the vitality of our seed, we might do well to imitate them, if only we knew how. But such an ideal will not induce men to restrain their appetites or to endure toil and danger. Though nature care only for the existence of the physical type, we ought to promote the 'good' life of individuals and be prepared to espouse a cause which in the struggle for existence may not be a certain winner.

(32) And so more recently a new turn has been given to the old maxim, and we are advised to learn from nature how to outwit her. No longer are we asked to accept her standard of mere survival, but, setting up our proper ideal of a higher life, to contrive by her own means of struggle and elimination that this shall be the survivor. For so I understand the doctrine of the superman, put forward with no great consistency by Nietzsche, a popular form of which may thus be summarized. The present race of men is so pitifully weak and stupid that our only duty is, by every means in our power, to intensify the struggle for existence and so weed out the unfit more rapidly, hoping that thus we may hasten the advent of a better race, perhaps as superior to ourselves as we to monkeys.

It is recognized that this account of duty does not square with either the ordinary or the Christian view. Its supporters have therefore gone on to describe the kinds of conduct characteristic of that superior race which we ought to try to produce as 'ruler virtues'. These would be hardness, ruthless determination, courage (combined I suppose with prudence), and, in general, 'efficiency'. And they are contrasted with the 'slave virtues' of pity, charity, patience, self-sacrifice, which damnify their possessors and preserve more incompetent persons. These latter ideals, it is suggested, have been foisted upon the strong by the weak for their own ends, yet they are, in fact, wrong; though if the strong were so stupid as to be taken in, we may perhaps think all was for the evolutionary best. In order to produce a race of 'rulers', those of us who possess some modicum of ruler-virtues ought apparently to develop them and assert ourselves by every means; yet those in whom the slave-virtues predominate ought surely to practise these, and by every kind of self-abnegation give place to the higher type. But the martyr to posterity who refused to survive on the ground that he was not fit has a quality that we would not willingly let die.

It is paradoxical to describe one who seeks only his own survival either as the ideal 'ruler' or as most beneficial to his race. We think the ideal captain is the one who sticks to his sinking ship, not a man who hides under the thwarts of the life-boat or even forces his way to it with a revolver before the women and children. Courage is good for the race, but the courage of the martyr rather than that of the hooligan. The world is only a tolerable place to live in, and would only be tolerable for the superman—unless he were a beast—by dint of forbearance, patience, sympathy, and justice. The upholders of the doctrine seem to mean that in the vegetable and animal worlds adaptation to environment results partly from the struggle for existence by the survival of the fittest. But of following nature in this sense we have seen the fallacy.

If the superman is to be superior to ourselves in the most important things, he will be more just, more merciful, more self-sacrificing. And to eliminate these qualities in his progenitors is a doubtful policy for producing him. Ability to survive is no test of goodness unless we think that the process of the world is designed and guided to secure the survival of goodness. Would the true superman, being juster and more humane than ourselves, thank us for producing him by cruelty and injustice? If he were the kind of creature to do so, the duty of sacrificing anything for his production will be vainly urged upon me. Mere power is no more an adequate ideal for moral efforts than was mere life. The production of a superman is not an end of such a kind that it is our duty to do anything whatever that might conduce to it. It remains to inquire if any other such end can be found.

Note. Biological evolution differs essentially from the metaphorical evolution of knowledge, opinions, and tastes. Physical characteristics can only be transmitted to offspring and, therefore, tend to disappear, if adverse to survival. The knowledge how to make anaesthetics, the opinion that their use is wrong, the taste for opium, can all be transmitted to anybody willing to accept them. They may, therefore, survive, though adverse to survival. Celibacy may survive. One reason that makes beliefs acceptable is if the arguments for them are sound.

IV

UTILITARIANISM

(33) IF, then, we seem driven to suppose that our duty is to bring about not mere survival but some *good* kind of life for men, the simplest suggestion will be that this consists in their happiness. And here we should find ready to our hands a formula, that of the Greatest Happiness of the Greatest Number, which has perhaps had a greater influence on popular theories of morality than any other.

It was a misfortune for the doctrine of Utilitarianism that it was often supposed, as by its eloquent exponent John Mill, to be capable of some connexion with hedonism and even with psychological hedonism, till Henry Sidgwick tried to rescue it from this entanglement. And yet it no doubt owed some of its vogue to this really discreditable and falsely alleged relation. If we have succeeded in showing that men desire other things besides pleasure and do not always think that they ought to seek pleasure, it is at least not self-evident that their greatest pleasure is the only thing we can owe them. Still, it would be an intelligible, even an attractive statement, that, though men have vagrant and turbulent desires, yet if they were prudently selfish they would subordinate all these to their greatest happiness, and that it is our duty to satisfy the selfish prudence of all impartially.

(34) I refrain at present from the question whether a man can have duties other than to his neighbours, for these, if there be any duty, are indisputable. Why, we must ask then, should we allot happiness impartially,

and what does impartially mean? It can only mean justly; and, whether that implies equally or in proportion to desert, it is hard to see how this duty is consistent with utilitarianism. If our only obligation be to produce happiness, then we can have no obligation to do justice also, except as a means to greater quantities of happiness. Much wit has accordingly been spent to prove that just division of happiness usually results in a larger sum total of the dividend.

(1) When *justly* is taken to mean *equally* it has been said that men are rendered so uneasy by envying the superior fortune of others that their uneasiness always more than counterbalances the greater pleasure of the more favoured. This is not so with all natures, for we often observe a simple pleasure taken in contemplating the life of those in superior stations which are thought of as a source of pleasure to their occupants. The old and feeble enjoy the spectacle of youth and vigour. And most men feel a very keen displeasure at equality when industry during the heat of the day meets with no better reward than do the idle and shiftless. So far as men do attach importance to equality it is in great measure because they think that in some respects, and so far as it depends on human agency, men *should* be treated equally; that is, they make precisely the moral judgement of the intrinsic rightness of justice—whether it produce a greater total of pleasure or not—which utilitarianism is bound to deny.

(35) (2) When *justly* is taken to mean *in accordance with merit* utilitarians have used two arguments to reconcile it with their doctrine.

(*a*) The first identifies merit with expectation. If by a bargain, explicit or implied, I have led some one to expect a benefit from me, then, even if another need that benefit more, the disappointment of the creditor must be weighed against the other's greater need. But it is only *just* expectations—founded, say, on promises made by me or work done for me—that I feel bound to fulfil, not those of grasping heirs or sanguine burglars. So the obligation to justice is assumed in the very argument that pretends to resolve it into a greater quantity of pleasure.

(36) (*b*) The second argument for the same purpose is closely connected with the first. It identifies the reward of merit with the encouragement of utilitarian conduct. We should be honest and keep *our* contracts, and indeed give gratuities for service rendered—even when we might produce more immediate happiness by spending the money otherwise—because mankind is much concerned in the *general* habit of keeping contracts, and our example will strengthen the custom. The only reason, then, for not robbing Peter to please Paul (taking Paul's pleasure to be greater than Peter's pain) is that it might encourage others to rob Paul to please Peter when Paul's pain is greater than Peter's pleasure. The only reason for paying my creditor when I need the money more than he does is that otherwise my example may lead rich men to cheat the poor. To this argument two answers may be given.

(1) The first is that it assumes a very remarkable stupidity in men. They are told both that the only right conduct is to try to produce the greatest happiness, and also that they must perform the act called paying a debt, even when it manifestly does not produce the greatest happiness, for fear they should encourage people not to perform it when it manifestly does. It is

like telling us to confer improper favours for fear we should encourage ourselves or others to refuse proper ones.

(2) Our second reply will be that this utilitarian excuse for doing just acts, even if that directly produce less happiness than not doing them, on the ground of their value as example, assumes that the acts are public. Consequently, however solemnly we might have promised a dying creditor to pay his children, yet, if nobody knew of the debt and if we honestly believed that we could make more happiness by breaking our word, it would be our plain duty to break it. The promise would simply count for nothing. And we should never reward the faithful rather than the vicious unless we were sure either that the former valued money more or that our generosity would be seen of men. We should never *owe* anything to anybody. In short, it seems impossible for a consistent utilitarian to find any place for our inexpugnable belief in the rightness of keeping some promises, paying some debts, and rewarding some merits even when more happiness might be produced by not doing these acts. For a utilitarian the individual and his claims are of no peculiar value, but must be sacrificed absolutely to the happiness of the majority. If we thought the torture of a few victims increased the sum of happiness we should think it right. And if we could produce more pleasure for a thoroughly selfish and cruel man than for any one else, that would be our bounden duty.

(37) To say, then, that our duty is to give as much pleasure as possible is a definition both too wide and too narrow. We do not think we ought to give every kind of pleasure to everybody and we think we ought

to give some people some things other than their greatest pleasure. And we think our distribution of satisfaction should be *just*. Our proper debts to our parents, our children, our friends, our country, our creditors, are not merely opportunities for affording more pleasure to these parties than we could at the moment give to others. They are particular obligations. I myself, when on the mountains, feel a much stronger obligation to make away with my own lunch-paper than with that left there by the profane, though one causes as much pain as the other. But here I may be wrong.

(38) It may be best at this point to indicate the element of truth which, I believe, utilitarianism contains, and which gives it its plausibility, though the reasons for my belief must be postponed. I think, though I am not so confident of this as of anything that I have yet said, that every right act must afford some satisfaction to somebody. I mean satisfaction other than (and prior to) the satisfaction of a right act having been done. Of course it does not follow that the act which gives the greatest quantity of satisfaction is, as the utilitarians hold, the right one. Some satisfactions are *due*, are in the circumstances the ones we ought to give; others not.

I confess to finding a difficulty for this view in the case where, to soothe a dying man, I had promised him something which could be no cause of satisfaction to anybody, as to bury him in some peculiar spot. Opinions as to the degree of obligation here might differ, but it clearly tends to disappear in proportion as the promise involves positive loss of satisfaction to others, as would a promise to bury his unpublished poems or scientific discoveries with him. I have to admit that I should not myself feel the obligation of such a promise strongly. Probably, in proportion to my regard for the dead, I should keep it, as others might heap his coffin with flowers, as an excusable relief to my feelings. Perhaps here I am corrupted by theory, but, to forestall the gibes of misology, I may remark that it is also theory which leads me to suspect my corruption. Most 'plain men' are full of theory which they never suspect. I cannot help thinking of such a promise as one made to a man suffering from a delusion from which, on any hypothesis as to immortality, he is now free. Of course a promise to give some satisfaction to others might be binding, though this satisfaction would bring none to the dead man. Whether I ought to have made the promise is a different question.

(39) If an action cannot be right unless it afford somebody some satisfaction, *a fortiori* it follows that utilitarians are also correct in maintaining that we must consider the 'consequences of action'. Those who have said that we can judge an 'action' right or wrong without considering 'consequences' have in fact always considered some consequences of our bodily movement, though they arbitrarily include these in the 'act' itself, and refused to consider others, to which they arbitrarily confine the name 'consequences'. For instance, some have held that we know it is wrong to lie and neither need nor should consider the consequences. But in calling my 'action' a lie I have already considered some consequences of moving my tongue, namely, that there are persons within hearing who will be misled by what I say. Otherwise to tell a fairy story, even to oneself, would be a lie. And if I must go so far into the

future as to consider whether anybody may be deceived by my words, it is hard to see why I should not go further and consider the consequences of the deception, as for instance that it may prevent a crime or a disaster.

The mistake of the utilitarians was not that they considered consequences, but that they only considered some consequences (namely pleasures), and considered nothing else but consequences. We must also consider the antecedents. Whether I ought to initiate a certain change in a given situation depends upon what that situation is. Whether I ought to pay a sum of money to A or B depends not only upon whether A's or B's possession of it will result in more pleasure, but on whether A or B is my creditor, my government, my parent, my benefactor or a stranger, and upon how they and I have behaved in the past.

(40) Another difficulty urged against utilitarians is the same which beset the hedonists. If pleasure is the only thing we owe to others, then it is its quantity only and not its quality which we must consider. We ought only to spread a taste for music and poetry, instead of beer and skittles, so far as we are assured that the aesthetic pleasures are keener, less mixed, and more permanent. If the utilitarian grant that to enjoy Homer and Shakespeare is 'better' than to enjoy the serio-comic and the moving pictures, he seems to admit a 'good' which he ought to produce but which is assessed by something else than an amount of pleasure.

And it would be difficult for him to convince us that, in certain circumstances, we ought not to improve people's taste, though we were not sure that this would increase their pleasure on the whole. Yet for a consistent utilitarian to spend energy on educating others, by a painful process, to share his preferences would be an intolerant persecution. On his principle unpopular art means bad art or, at least, art which should be discouraged. For surely Homer has caused less pleasure, at the cost of greater pain, than many 'best sellers'.

(41) In criticizing hedonism we suggested [1] that, even if it were possible to subordinate all other motives to the desire for the maximum of pleasure, many men might not choose to do so. If this be true, then, as we said at the beginning, utilitarianism loses its prima facie plausibility.[2] For if men sometimes choose something other than happiness, it is possible that we ought to give them something else. An argument of this kind is often used against utilitarianism in a form which seems to me mistaken, but which has led to the substitution of another definition of right conduct, which we must next consider. In criticizing that definition we shall see what the mistake is.

The form of argument is that utilitarianism recognizes a duty to give others a 'good',[3] and one good only, namely pleasure. To do this duty, it is said, is to be 'good' and must therefore be the 'good' of the agent. Yet, the argument goes on, it seems irrational that one man's 'good' should differ fundamentally from another's. Ought we not then perhaps to give to others that 'good' which we ought to choose for ourselves, namely, the 'goodness' of being 'good' which we have recognized as 'our good'? Should we not make others better, or need we only treat them like pet animals and make them comfortable?

[1] § 25. [2] § 33.

[3] For the ambiguity of the term *good* see § 58.

V

PERFECTIONISM

(42) It is suggested, then, in the next place that our duty to others may be to improve them, to induce in them right conduct and better character, which will naturally be accompanied by 'higher' pleasures and 'higher' pains in exchange for 'lower' pleasures and pains which they will escape. We should then in right action produce the same 'good' for them which we secure for ourselves, namely, moral goodness and virtue. To this doctrine the name of perfectionism has been sometimes given, and, though it is not very happy, I keep it rather than invent another.

This is not, I think, a very important theory, and can be dealt with shortly, though it suggests some important distinctions. It would perhaps never have been formulated except as an amendment to utilitarianism, being similarly one-sided but in the opposite direction. That it is often our duty to make other people in some sense better, as it often is to give them pleasure, I should not deny, but only that it covers *all* our duties.

(43) Various critics have condemned the alleged duty of improving others as being (1) vague, (2) impossible, and (3) useless. Utilitarians say it is *vague* because we have no agreed recipe for goodness, whereas every one knows how to get pleased; and *useless* because if the goodness we are to promote consists, like our own, in improving others whose goodness is to improve others again, nobody is ever the 'better off' for this endless circulation of a paper currency which is never cashed. A more rigorous school, defining morality as the self-

determined effort at right action in spite of temptation and difficulty (a view to be considered later), deny the *possibility* of making others morally better.

(44) (1) Of the first objection we may say that even if it were more difficult to know how to make a man good than happy it still might be our duty to try. But the perfectly definite and tangible character ascribed to happiness may be questioned. No two persons take their pleasure in quite the same things; and even if we confined our attention to the elementary conditions of happiness necessary for all men—sufficient food, shelter, work, and leisure, though our energies might be occupied our path would not be clear. Our aim being the greatest happiness of the greatest number, we must take account of an infinity of future generations. May not increased comfort increase the number of competitors? Is more happiness secured in the end by equal distribution or by gradation? by discipline or by freedom? How far should effort be stimulated by competition? The material side of social reform is not without its problems. After all, happiness depends much on temperament and the beggar may be happier than the squire. We might be less at a loss to prescribe the education which would make a child good than for one that would make it happy. The only truth of the objection is that to give an immediate pleasure is easy. But pleasures interfere with one another and one of them may cause greater pain in the end to the recipient or to other persons. To make even a slight improvement in a man's character is hard, but once made it is not likely to interfere with his virtue for the future or with that of others.

(45) (2) The second objection, that to make others

better is impossible, depends upon an important ambiguity in the word *good*. A good man may mean (*a*) a *moral* man (that is, one who does whatever he believes right and does it for that reason, however mistaken he may be, and however much tempted to do something different). In this sense it is perhaps impossible to make others good. We cannot even prove to them that they should be. We could only show them the policy, here or hereafter, of honesty, or arouse virtuous desires, or point out duties they had overlooked. And in none of these three ways should we make them more moral. Every man must acquire his own merit, which is only decreased when the path of duty is painted in primrose colours or temptations are removed.

A man who, with inherited temperament, education, and surroundings all against him, makes great efforts and advances even a little way, is *morally* worthier than one who starts on a level of virtue (for which he is not responsible) higher than the other ever reached, yet makes no effort to rise further.

(*b*) Or a good man, secondly, might mean one who does what actually is right; and this we may at least make possible for him by training him in ethical discriminations and enlightening him about the consequences of his acts and the circumstances of his situation. We may even make it easy by decreasing his temptations.

(*c*) For lastly a good man may mean what I should call a *virtuous* man, that is, one with good desires—desires to do kinds of acts which are generally right. Certainly we can do something towards making people inclined to pity, courage, temperance, honesty, and inaccessible to gross and mean temptations. A perfectly virtuous man would always do right actions from love of them and from no sense of duty, but then he would no more be moral, in the narrow sense, than God is, to whose nature immorality is impossible.

Owing to these ambiguities I think it is usually better to avoid the term *good* in ethics. But this theory could hardly be stated without it, depending, as I believe it does, on those very ambiguities. I have therefore used inverted commas where I am uncertain of the meaning.

(46) (3) We are now better able to consider the force also of the last objection, namely, that to improve others is useless. If it were true both that our only duty is to make others 'good' and also that the only way for them to be 'good' is to do what they think right (namely, make others good) as against desire, certainly the sacrifice of our own pleasure to duty would bring about nothing except that others should sacrifice theirs to the same. There is, I think, no *logical* absurdity in this. But it does seem to travesty our moral judgements for the reasons given above: that there are other things than morality which we sometimes think ought to be secured for others and that their morality cannot be secured by us. And yet among the activities we think should be exercised both by ourselves and others, a high place must be retained, at least in the world as we know it, by that of 'self-sacrifice', the denial of a selfish interest for some interest of others, of pleasure for duty. I hope some of these confusions may be diminished when the situation is stated less vaguely.

VI

SELF-SACRIFICE AND SELF-REALIZATION

(47) RIGHT conduct has been popularly identified with self-sacrifice. But what is sacrificed must, by the meaning of the word, have some value, and sacrifice can therefore only be chosen as a means to the realization of something with a greater value. Such is the ordinary statement of the antithesis; it seems to mean that we should sacrifice satisfactions, which have a hedonistic value, for the sake of doing what is right, which has a moral value. To sacrifice one's own capacities or happiness for absolutely no reason, real or imaginary, might be called either wicked or stupid: really, I think, the action is not conceivable. To take *pleasure* in the infliction of pain on oneself or others is insanity. Not even the insane would purposely pain themselves if they thought it would be no good or pleasure to others or themselves.

> Self-love, my liege, is not so vile a sin
> As self-neglecting.[1]

Right conduct, then, commonly involves the sacrifice of something we cannot help *wanting* for something *right* with which it is incompatible. And this is meritorious in proportion to the sacrifice it entails. In a perfect being, who had no desires inconsistent with doing right, sacrifice would have no place. But in human life it involves self-realization. For however much we sacrifice our desires it is always to realize our own ideals and in obedience to our own convictions, if only

[1] Shakespeare, *Henry V*, II. iv.

to acquire that habitual mastery over impulse which we think we ought to get. Asceticism is only training.

(48) Thus it is that right conduct has also been plausibly defined as Self-realization. Such a theory is of course meant to be no defence of selfishness. It professes to start from an obligation, reasonably recognized, to develop our faculties, to widen our sympathies, to extend our experience and knowledge to the utmost.

It is hardly likely to be questioned that such self-development often falls among our duties and, indeed, among our duties to our neighbours. But at other times it is as clearly right to postpone our own physical, intellectual, and aesthetic culture, even perhaps our own innocence and sensitiveness, to the claims of other men. That, too, it may be claimed, is still self-realization. But in this sense clearly no act can be done which does not realize some capacity of the self by sacrificing some other capacity. It will be replied that the right act, or the act which the agent believes right, always realizes a more fundamental self, and that those who think to realize themselves by selfishness, however ambitious and refined, are mistaken. Such an argument seems to be circular. Asking what we ought to do, we are told to realize ourselves. Asking what sort of acts achieve this, we are told, 'The ones we ought to do'.

(49) Indeed, the formula would perhaps not have survived reflection had it not been the grindstone for a metaphysical axe. Its most considerable champions claim that it is not the empirical, individual self, distinguished from other selves and exclusive of them, which we should realize, but the universal self or reason in which we all share and which, as absolute or *noumenon*, lies behind the phenomenal appearance of indivi-

duality. What we in fact have to realize is God; yet the absolute is by definition real already, no mere potentiality or capacity of appearances; and it includes both good and evil, or rather both of these are ways in which it appears. I am not sure whether it is the doing of what we, to some extent mistakenly, think right, or of what, though perhaps we do not know it, actually is right, which would be held to realize or satisfy the universal reason. At all events it is not the universal self which does my acts, unless we think it does some acts which do not satisfy itself, namely, my bad acts. Again, since the empirical, acting self really does appear to have 'selfish', bad desires, which are just what distinguish it from the universal 'self', it would be as reasonable to adopt the language of some Christian moralists and, lumping all these angry or concupiscent impulses together under the name of 'self' (as the idealists did the promptings of reason), to proclaim that right conduct is the sacrifice of this self to the will of God. For though we often feel that our temptations assail us from without, yet the guilt of yielding is our own, and conscience, too, has often seemed an inspiration or grace given. The truest self is that which chooses ill or well. At any rate, when a man does his duty to his neighbour he is no more aiming at self-realization than at his own pleasure. He is not generally thinking about pleasing God. It may be that all these results will follow, but neither the desire for them nor a sense of obligation to produce them is his motive, and they would not follow unless his motive were the belief that the act was right. What he is thinking about is doing the right thing, and the right thing in a given situation may be sacrificing what seems to him the development of himself to that of another. Self-realization is a less crudely cynical theory than hedonism, but its fallacy is the same. And to avoid crudity is not always to escape misunderstanding. There is a well-found story of an Oriental at a congress of religions who summed up his paper in these words; 'Conclusion is: Christianity no good for fighting nation. So hurrah! for Sir Bradley and self-realization.'

(50) A similar *arrière-pensée* for the metaphysical distinction between appearance and absolute reality has sometimes led to the suggestion that the principles of self-realization and self-sacrifice are both indefeasibly valid, with equal claims upon our obedience, so that they clash in an internecine conflict which admits of no rational solution, but only of a practical compromise whose result can be nothing but a makeshift. The conclusion drawn from this is that morality belongs to the world of appearance and contradiction, not to that of rational reality.

Such metaphysical quarrels it is not the business of moral philosophy to compose. But I have never been able to see the peculiar irrationality of the conflict which arises between the duties of self-development and the others. Suppose nothing but self-development were in question; yet my physical and mental well-being, each an excellent thing in itself, might conflict, since it is hard to be a first-rate athlete, or even a first-class life, and also an assiduous scholar. Within the mental field itself art and philosophy are often found incompatible. Similarly, if I devote myself wholly to the good of others and treat my own development entirely as a means to that, I may have to choose between their mental and physical improvement, and, in either choice, sacrifice something I should gladly have secured, and ought to have secured had both been possible. If the contention amount to no more than this: that no single act can satisfy all the desires I have or fulfil all the duties which at other times and in other circumstances I might have, and that no finite being in a limited life can achieve all the ideals he can conceive, the point may be allowed. Perfection is for God, to whom we cannot ascribe moral choice.[1] But on a given occasion, though there may be conflicting desires, I can only have one duty.[2] If that duty is 'realized' incompatible desires are sacrificed to it; the result may approximate to a harmony of the whole self, so far as the desires are gradually disciplined, but another sort of harmony may also be approached so far as conscience is atrophied and all desires enslaved to selfish prudence.

(51) The difficulty of all these discussions between utilitarianism and perfectionism, self-realization and self-sacrifice, seems to arise from false abstraction. We have already noticed the utilitarian fallacy of speaking about pleasure as though it were separable from the acts in which it is taken or the means by which it is produced. But the same error is made on the opposite side when, for instance, it is said that 'we should choose virtue even if it brought no pleasure'.[3] It is impossible to conceive of a virtuous or of a moral act, or indeed of any act, which brought *no* satisfaction to the doer, and, as I have already said, it is hard to find a duty towards others, the performance of which will not bring *some* satisfaction to others. The moral action may not be the one I think will bring the greatest possible satisfaction

[1] See § 45 (*c*). [2] See § 84.

[3] Aristotle, *Ethics*, X. iii. 12.

to me or to others, but, if I think about satisfaction at all, I think it will bring some to both, namely, to me the satisfaction of doing my duty and to them the satisfaction which is due to them from me. But since neither their satisfaction nor mine need be the greatest possible in the circumstances, it is not the satisfactoriness (either for them or me) which makes the act seem right.

Similarly it has been said: 'Were there no use possibly to be made of it, no happiness which could possibly be promoted, generous and self-forgetting action would be worth having in the universe.'[1] But unless the writer meant that the agent mistakenly supposed such results to be possible I fail to understand him. One cannot act generously if one can find nothing that anybody wants, and self-forgetfulness, when there was nothing else practicable to remember, would be simply self-neglecting.

(52) I believe, then, that an act cannot be right unless it also have some utilitarian or, as it is sometimes called, economic value, that is, unless it give somebody some satisfaction; though some other act than the right one might have produced greater satisfaction. An act of mine, then, would not be moral (i. e. done because it is thought right), and have the value which moral acts have, unless I thought that it would give somebody some satisfaction. Yet moral acts have this value in themselves and not merely as means to some satisfactions, otherwise their value would be proportionate to the satisfaction produced or intended to be produced.[2] The doing of a right act which is not also either moral (i. e. done because it is thought right) or virtuous (i. e.

[1] J. Grote, *Treatise on the Moral Ideals*, ch. vi, p. 76. Almost a paraphrase from Kant.

[2] Cf. § 38.

done from a kind of desire that usually leads to right action) seems to have little value. Yet the whole value of a moral act depends upon the belief that it is really right. The distinction implied by Grote and also in the question whether the end justifies the means is another false abstraction. For it cannot be right to bring anything about irrespective of all possible cost to ourselves or others and of the rightness of incurring that cost. We can no doubt distinguish within the whole action the elements on which its rightness depends; for instance, the rightness of sparing pain even by saying what is not true, or the rightness of telling the truth even when it causes pain. But unless we use question-begging terms such as murder (that is, wrongful killing), I doubt if we can say that there is any 'end' which would justify every means or any 'means' which no end would justify. It is really the whole action that we judge, including all its foreseen consequences. Grote is wrong in suggesting that if we consider no quality of an act except its painfulness to the agent we can still judge it right. Any plausibility that his statement may have is derived either from our reaction against the opposite abstraction of his utilitarian opponents (that acts are right in proportion to the pleasure they produce), or from the truth that, if an action done because it is *judged right on other grounds* be also painful to the agent, this increases, not indeed its rightness or its morality, but its merit or desert. Simple pain satisfies nobody who has it, but an act done in spite of its painfulness because it is right gives a moral satisfaction which would not have been given had the act been pleasant.

An analogy from art may illustrate both of these false

abstractions at once. To praise a work of art while admitting that it gave no pleasure or satisfaction would be absurd. It would be no less absurd to praise it on the ground that it gave a greater quantity of pleasure than could have been secured in any other way with the same pains. It would be absurd to say that we endure the painful element in a tragedy as a mere means to a pleasurable element which we should prefer to get in some other way. The two are inseparable. The tragic pleasure is the pleasure in tragedy, absolutely conditioned by its pain, and the whole is 'worth having in the universe'. The pleasure of exercise is *in* the effort. The palm is nothing without the dust. Merit, like tragedy, implies both dissatisfaction and satisfaction. But not all beauty is tragic nor all right conduct meritorious. Both imply some satisfaction, but that is not their essence.

VII

THE COMMON GOOD

(53) IT would seem to have been chiefly in the effort to escape the abstract oppositions of self-sacrifice to self-realization, of hedonism to utilitarianism, and of these last two to perfectionism, that there was developed the next theory we have to consider. This holds that right action is that which conduces to 'the common good', a good which is said to be shared by the agent with the patient and indeed with all men, a good whose nature prevents it from being the object of rivalry. Such a view seems to be a more elaborate form of the one which we criticized under the name of Perfectionism. But the elaboration introduces new difficulties without removing the old. I have tried to lead the way to an understanding of this formula in the two preceding sections. The statement of it is undoubtedly more attractive at first sight than any view we have so far considered, and it has had a wide influence, but its precise meaning remains to me so obscure that I must give up the plan of stating it in my own words and substitute instances of the application of the term. These are taken from one of the ablest exponents of the theory, T. H. Green. I have italicized some words that seem to me crucial and inserted brief comments in square brackets. In his *Prolegomena to Ethics* he says: 'The only good in the pursuit of which there can be no competition of interests, the only good which is really common to all who may *pursue* it, is that which *consists in the universal will to be good*—in the settled disposition on each man's part to make the most and best of humanity in

his own person and in the persons of others' (244). This ideal 'is unrealized because the good is being sought in objects that admit of being competed for'. 'Until the object generally sought as good comes to be a state of mind or character of which the attainment, or approach to attainment, by each is itself a contribution to its attainment by every one else, social life must continue to be one of war' (245). [If by 'state of mind or character' be meant the good will, it is hard to see how my good will is a contribution to every one else's. The statement would be plausible of happiness if we were sufficiently sympathetic.] 'What is *the will for true good*? . . . It is the will to know what is true, to make what is beautiful; to endure pain and fear, to resist the allurements of pleasure' (256). [Then knowledge e. g. would be a true good, incapable of being competed for, besides 'the universal will to be good'.]

'The good has come to be conceived with increasing clearness, *not as anything which one man or set of men can gain or enjoy to the exclusion of others*, but as a spiritual activity in which all may partake, and in which all must partake, if it is to amount to a full realization of the faculties of the human soul, . . . a perfecting of man, which is itself conceived not as an external end to be obtained by goodness, but as *consisting in such a life of self-devoted activity* on the part of all persons' (286). [Perfection of the race is certainly unobtainable until all men are perfect. But how can my exercise of 'self-devoted activity' depend on that of others?]

'There is no real reason to doubt that the good or evil in the motive of an action is exactly measured by the good or evil in its consequences' (295). [If this were so, we ought not to care how ignorant our rulers were if they meant well. It seems to imply that what anybody thinks right is right or at least useful.] 'No one, except under constraint of some extravagant theory, denies that pleasure is good' (368). We must 'think of the perfect life as essentially *conditioned* by the exercise of virtues, resting on a self-sacrificing will, in which it is open to all men to participate, and as fully attainable by one man only in so far as through those virtues it is attained by all' (370). [Apparently the virtues of self-sacrifice which condition the good life are non-competitive goods. But they may be fully attainable by one though not attained by others. The other elements of a perfect life, conditioned by virtue (pleasure e.g. and knowledge), may be competitive. The attainment of these latter goods by one sometimes depends on the possession of the *other* good (self-sacrifice) by others.]

Finally, we are told that 'in thinking of ultimate good' a civilized man 'thinks of it indeed necessarily as perfection for himself; as a life in which he shall be *fully satisfied* through having become all that the spirit within him enables him to become. But he cannot think of himself as satisfied in any life other than a social life, exhibiting the exercise of a *self-denying will* and in which "the multitude of the redeemed", which is all men, shall participate. He has other faculties indeed than those which are directly exhibited in the specifically moral virtues—faculties which find their expression not in his dealings with other men, but in the arts and sciences—and the development of these must also be a necessary constituent in any life which he presents to himself as one in which he can find satisfaction. But "when he sits down in a calm hour" it will not be in isolation that the development of any of these faculties will assume the character for him of ultimate good' (370). [Just because men are not isolated their full satisfactions or intellectual perfections conflict and some sometimes ought to be sacrificed: but I cannot think of myself as at once 'fully satisfied' and 'exercising a self-denying will'.]

As 'a criterion of what is good or bad in law and usage and in the tendencies of men's actions' we are offered this: 'Does this or that law or usage, this or that course of action—directly or indirectly, positively or as a preventive of the opposite—contribute to the better-being of society, as measured by the more general establishment of conditions favourable to the attainment of the recognized excellences and virtues, by the more general attainment of those excellences in some degree, or by their *attainment on the part of some persons in higher degree* without detraction from the opportunities of others?' [Here it seems we need not consider if the law or action produce pleasure—which 'no one denies is good'—or if it be just, but only if it promote the virtue of others. And it seems that some persons *can* attain virtue without others attaining it, or even by detraction from the opportunities of others, which before was denied] (354, 371).

'No one can gain directly in intrinsic worth by the action of another' (316). [Then, if he be more virtuous than he would have been had we not established conditions favourable to self-sacrifice, has he gained indirectly? Or has he only gained the *goods* called pleasure or knowledge which carry *no intrinsic worth*?]

'While the loss of pleasure *implied in* the sacrifice to the person who makes it, and to any others he can induce willingly to accept any like loss that arises out of it for them, is morally or relatively to the true good indifferent', the sacrifice *is* an undoubted contribution to human good (376). [Pleasure is a good, but its loss is morally indifferent; indeed the sacrifice of it *is* (not produces) a good, but only, we must suppose, if it is intended to produce some other good.]

In his *Principles of Political Obligation* Green says that we can have no rights except as members of a society which recognizes a common good as that which should be for each member, and that any one capable of being determined by a common good (i.e. every moral person) is capable of rights (25). [Here evidently a common good is something which should be, but may not be, possessed by each, and is apparently exactly similar for each.]

(54) On a survey of these passages I am driven to conclude that the term 'common good' is used in at least two different senses, on whose confusion the theory, as it is stated, depends.

(1) The simplest meaning of the terms 'common good' and 'common goods' would be a thing or things which can be used or owned in common, as land where various persons have the right to cut peat or pasture cattle. Such common ownership or 'user' is often said to be the most frequent source of quarrel, and is certainly not exempt from rivalry or competition. There is usually an assumed reasonable amount, equal or unequal, for each; and over this arise those disputes which private ownership might seem intended to remedy.

Doubtless all wish the common wealth to be great, but domestic politics are mainly the dispute about the proper division of the dividend and of the productive labour. In this kind of instance common ownership might be defined as the right to a voice in disputes about individual enjoyment. The peat I cut is not the peat you cut, and even when I have kindled it on my 'common hearth', different rays warm different people, and my family may compete for the ingle-nook. Even 'the common air' is a misnomer, only plausible so long as there is more than enough for all. If we each want to see the same scene or picture we shall crowd one another out. If good be satisfaction or enjoyment, then my good can never be yours, and there is no common good. If good be a source of satisfaction or an object of desire, then there is clearly a sense in which an event or a condition of things may be *desired* by us both; but what can be *enjoyed* by us is not the event or the condition, but our individual awareness of it, and that may be an object of competition. We must distinguish the desires of two soldiers that their country should win from the desire of each to survive and witness that victory, which might be a matter of rivalry.[1] So, when Green says that right action is that which conduces to the common good, does he mean that we should try to bring about that and only that which we desire to happen and which many or all others desire to happen also? Perhaps he might also mean, though he would have stated his meaning loosely, that we should try to get what we desire when and only when that involves bringing about what some or all others desire also. When two friends desire one another's company, I think that it cannot be strictly said that they desire the same thing, any more than if they both desired solitude; but their desires cannot, so far, conflict. If this be what Green means I think it is not true. Neither the fact

[1] Cf. 'A life in which he shall be fully satisfied' (p. 59).

(*a*) that a great many people desire an event which I desire and that nobody desires anything inconsistent with it, nor the fact (*b*) that the satisfaction of my desire will involve the satisfactions of other people's desires and no dissatisfactions, seems a *necessary* condition of my act being right. For I often think it right to do things which I do not want to do and which most other people do not want me to do. Whether either of those conditions, (*a*) or (*b*), if it could be fulfilled, would be *sufficient* to make an act right is not worth discussing. For, if everybody wanted me to do what I myself wanted to do, I think that the question of duty would not arise.

If, then, by 'promoting the common good' Green mean bringing about the satisfaction of all or several persons including myself and the dissatisfaction of none, as a definition of right action this will not do.

(55) (2) But there is a quite different sense in which we may speak of a 'good' 'common to' various individuals and by its very nature uniting them. We may mean something which they all agree in *judging right*; for instance, a just distribution; or any relation of one party to the other, or any condition of any one, which they all think ought to be established or maintained.[1] The confusion of these two senses of the term is disastrous. We must not assume that because a system of free state-education is 'a common good' in either sense it also is in the other. We might all agree to think it should be maintained though it could not be enjoyed by all and was not desired by all. Though it could be

[1] The question whether we judge anything good, in the sense that it ought to be, as distinct from merely satisfying somebody, except a moral or a right act, will be discussed in Ch. VIII.

enjoyed by all (subject, of course, to disputes) we might think it ought to be abolished, perhaps just because it could be enjoyed by all irrespective of means or capacities. Free beer, even if enjoyed and desired by all, need not be thought right by all to supply. If we agreed on the propriety of unemployment-doles they would be a common good in that sense, but not as being enjoyed by all. I may well approve of something being done by which I cannot myself profit. If I approve an act, the knowledge that it is done will doubtless satisfy me morally, but perhaps less than something inconsistent with the doing of it would have satisfied me in another way.

(56) But in this sense of Common Good—that which we all think right as opposed to what satisfies us—the formula that we ought to promote the Common Good clearly tells us nothing, or at least nothing true, about right action. It either tells us that we ought to do what is right, if we can only find out what it is; and that we knew already. Or it tells us that we ought to do what (and only what) all men think right, if we can discover any such action; and that is untrue. If the common good be that all private goods should be distributed rightly, it remains to inquire what those 'goods' are, what is a right distribution, and how agreement on these points may be attained. Yet in the other sense—a means of enjoyment which can be utilized by all persons—the rule of promoting the Common Good is quite unacceptable. It would lead us to think the provision of public games necessarily right and the distribution of bread wrong. Moreover, if the only Common Good be right or moral action, my right or moral action 'contributes' to it just in the sense of being an instance

of it. But if the Common Good be the satisfaction of all, my act is only the means of bringing it about.

Green has tried to avoid the opposition between the 'good' of the agent and the 'goods' of others, which we found in previous theories, not, as he should, by substituting for it the opposition between what is right (for anybody in the same circumstances) and what the agent desires, but by asserting that what is 'truly good' for one is always 'truly good' for all. In this he confuses three meanings of 'good', (1) satisfying, (2) right, (3) thought right. But (*a*) doing what I think wrong may give *most* satisfaction both to me and to others; certainly it often seems to me that it will. (*b*) It is only doing what I *think* right which gives me moral satisfaction, and this will give no moral satisfaction to others unless they know I did what I thought right. (*c*) Even then, they may think I thought and did wrong. Finally, if 'self-sacrificing will' be the only 'true good',[1] either right action is not good (if it involve no sacrifice) or right action is simply any sacrifice of desires which is thought right. If this were so we could never decide what *is* right. In order that the 'true good', which is self-sacrificing will, should be realized, far from it being necessary that all men should come to see that this is the only good, the very opposite seems required. In a perfectly satisfied world or a world of purely rational beings morality would have no place. If I am to be able to sacrifice myself to others both they and I must *want* (and in that sense think good) other things besides morality, and these must be competitive. Otherwise my sacrifice would be pointless and I should have nothing to sacrifice.

[1] See quotations above, pp. 57, 58, 59, 61.

(57) A more recent form of this theory has taken account of some of the criticisms brought against it, and presents it in a more guarded and less ambiguous form. Here we have an attempt to bring moral philosophy into line with the idealist theory that fact is created by thinking and consists in coherent thought. We are now told that goodness is created by willing and consists ultimately in coherent willing; and willing has two species, desiring and acting. On this view things, such as food, poison, tools, have a derivative goodness if they satisfy or enable us to satisfy our will. But the willing, from which other things derive goodness, is itself more or less good in proportion as it is 'coherent'. Desires and acts are coherent so far as they 'fit in with' a reflective 'policy' and are not disconnected impulses. So far, then, the man who deliberately dedicates his life with great self-restraint and pertinacity to a calculated revenge is good, and what he does is good. The pain of his victim is 'good for him'. He is better than one who hits out in resentment, repents, apologizes, and, when the irritation recurs, hits again. But there is a further stage. Willing only attains that high degree of coherence called rightness when it fits in with the policies of other men: if with that of some group of men with whom 'we will to co-operate' (say, our fellow robbers or fellow countrymen), it appears to be rather right; if of all men (living or past and future as well), very right; if of all *good* men or the *ideal* man, quite right. And willing has the kind of goodness called moral when it is done because of such supposed agreement.

(58) We have seen [1] that the word *good* sometimes

[1] § 10.

means merely efficient and sometimes right or moral. 'A good burglar' is so called in the first sense; his act is wrong, and the utmost deliberation and perseverance increase its immorality while in no degree increasing its rightness. The goodness of a good man and a good burglar are neither species of a genus nor degrees of one quality. What seems to be meant is that the acts of the good burglar cohere among themselves, while those of the good man cohere also with the desires and policies of other people. But these are two different relations, as different as pleasing myself from pleasing others. They could only be called different degrees of one quality on the assumption that what every man most deliberately wants is to act in harmony with the wants of other people, so that the good burglar, though politic as compared with the irresolute burglar, is a creature of impulse compared with the honest man.

(59) But if we are to take seriously the contention that it is coherence which makes acts right, surely it must be actual coherence with actual desires and wills of actual people, every one to count for one, and not with ideal desires and wills or with some selected by what the upholders of this view call 'an arbitrary intuitive standard'. No doubt, so far as I and others act rightly our acts do not conflict. But to say that what makes acts right is their coherence with *right* acts is nugatory. Yet unless they say that, they reduce right conduct to a conformity with the ways of mankind, including among mankind the most barbarous times and races.

(60) Further, when we are told that willing creates goodness and goodness is coherence, we must ask whether a given act is in itself coherent with the desires and policies of other people, or only so far as it is willed

as being or in order to be so coherent. The first interpretation is inconsistent with holding that what makes anything good is the willing of it; for it would mean that coherence was good even when not willed. The second is open to all the objections against making the rightness of an act depend upon the intention or motive or spirit of the agent; for if an act is good or coherent when willed because it is thought coherent, why should the agent trouble to inquire if it really is coherent, or what could he mean by doing so? Finally, if the act is coherent or good or right simply in virtue of having been coherently willed, what is meant by willing it *as* coherent or good or right?

(61) Neither rightness of acts, nor morality of agents, nor merit in resisting temptations seems properly describable as being any kind of coherence. The elements of truth which give plausibility to such a theory have already been recognized. They are—

(1) That what is right for one is, in similar circumstances, right for all, so that true judgements about rightness never conflict.

(2) All right acts bring some satisfaction to somebody, and so 'cohere with' some desire,—not with will, for nobody else can will my acts.

(3) 'Duty' and 'right action' only hold for rational beings capable of recognizing them.

But perhaps the chief plausibility of the view arises from the ambiguity which makes us reluctant to say that a man has a duty to do what he does not, and perhaps cannot, know to be his duty. I take it the correct expression is that there may be acts right for him to do which he cannot know to be right and therefore cannot be blamed for not doing.

VIII
RIGHT AND GOOD

(62) We saw that it would be equally appropriate to describe the very same conduct as either self-sacrifice or self-realization. A similar conclusion might be drawn from our criticism of the rival formulas of utilitarianism, perfectionism, and common good. If the life of a St. Francis might be equally approved as making men better or happier, as self-realization or self-sacrifice, and as promoting the common good; and that of a Cesare Borgia might be equally condemned as causing pain or encouraging vice, as selfish or self-degrading, and as violating the common good; what is the value of these distinctions and discussions?

It is not surprising if the duties which might seem deducible from opposing theories of morality are externally similar. For these theories are not spun out of air; they are merely attempts to describe generally the particular deliverances of our moral consciousness, and would never have been accepted had they not borne some resemblance to the facts they profess to describe. We have, however, tried to show that none of these theories completely covers all the acts which we judge right. And even if all of them did cover all; even if the acts we judged right to do were precisely those which would cause the greatest pleasure and also precisely those which would cause the greatest moral improvement and most promote the common good, it would still need to be decided which, if any, of these consequences is our reason for judging the acts right. We are not asking what are the actual consequences of a right act, but whether any of these consequences constitute its rightness: the agent's pleasure, or the greatest pleasure of others, or their improvement, or the common good, or something different from all of these.

(63) Impatience with such attempts at accuracy arises from practical enthusiasm. Many utilitarians were more interested in political reform, many perfectionists more in improving character, than in moral philosophy. If they could gain these ends they were little interested in the true description of what they were doing. I am far from denying that their aims were more important than mine. If the alternative had to be accepted, it would doubtless be better to abolish the slave trade or provide good education than to define morality or rightness. For moral philosophy does not aim at making men better, but at clearing up our notions of goodness. The goodness of a man without any theory about goodness may be just as good as that of one who has found its correct description. His acts are just as likely to be both right and moral. If he alter his moral judgements, not because he comes to see that they were erroneous (through ignorance perhaps of the situation or the consequences), but merely to conform them to a description, the need for this alteration proves the description to have been incorrect. The theory is nothing but an attempt to describe the facts; and to tamper with them is to poison the wells of truth. Astronomy would be easy if we could adjust the celestial movements to our prediction. When we criticize a particular moral judgement as being inconsistent with a principle, it is ultimately with other particular judgements that our comparison must be made. For the principle may be an inaccurate generalization. So far as two

situations are alike in all relevant facts, of course similar acts ought to be done in both.[1]

Has, then, it may be asked, moral philosophy no practical value? Its primary value is the satisfaction of intellectual curiosity. Like the pure scientist the philosopher should seek nothing but truth. Yet his knowledge, like other things, has effects and often affects conduct indirectly. In the first place I suppose that the more a man reflects upon 'the moral law', apart from the casuistical attempt to tamper with his genuine moral judgements, the more he is likely to reverence it. And secondly, since men must philosophize, or at any rate have philosophized, about conduct, we are apt to pick up some crude philosophy, such as hedonism, and then, finding that it does not fit our moral judgements, pedantically to distort them into conformity. So a juror, convinced that he should only seek the greatest happiness of the greatest number, might connive at the exemplary punishment of an innocent man universally believed guilty of some cruel crime. Or a man, honestly believing that the only duty was to seek the 'common good' of moral beings, might take less trouble to spare the unnecessary pain of animals, at least if men would not know of his cruelty.

(64) The truth appears to be that the rightness of an act cannot be deduced, as all the preceding theories assumed, from the 'goodness' of the result, whether achieved or aimed at. None of these theories escaped the false distinction of means and end. Nearly all moralists since Plato have attempted, and none of them with success, to prove that certain acts are right, either the acts commonly thought right in their day or some

[1] Cf. § 84.

slightly emended code of their own. And this they have generally tried to do by deducing the act from the conception of a good or end which it is to achieve. But there is no such proof of moral judgements. You cannot prove to a man that he has duties, or should do his duty, or that justice is a duty, or that this act is just. All you can do is to give him fuller information of the consequences and antecedents of what he is doing and then ask him to agree with you that it is right or wrong. If he know the situation and consequences as well as you do and still differ, one of you must be wrong, yet there is no proof. All you can do is to get him to imagine the situation again and repeat the act of moral thinking with greater attention. What we thus immediately judge right is doubtless always the bringing about of some state of things. But the state we ought to bring about is not first judged to be best in any other sense than that it is the one we ought to bring about. If it came about by chance or necessity we should not always judge it specially good. If this seem paradoxical it may be elucidated by one or two examples.

We have already made use of the famous instance from Hume. A just act may consist in taking money from a poor good man and giving it to a bad rich one. If the transaction be secret and not exemplary, my opponents could only say that a bad rich creditor plus £50 is a better thing in the world than a poor good debtor plus £50. But we should not think this if he picked up the money in the street. The 'goodness' then seems to consist not in his having the money but in the rightness of paying it to him. The 'goodness' 'produced' by truth-telling may reside wholly in the telling of truth, which we cannot distinguish from its expected hearing by others. And here again the unambiguous word is 'rightness'. Or suppose two men to be in a situation where only one can be saved from starvation. We should think it wrong of *either* forcibly to kill the other, even if that other were admittedly somewhat less good and useful than himself. We should perhaps think it a right act of *either* to save the other by sacrificing himself, even if they knew themselves equal in all respects. Again, we might think it right to punish an unscrupulously cruel man without hoping either to reform him or to deter others; but I doubt if we should consider it 'good' that he should happen to have a painful disease. In none of these instances does it seem possible to say that the act is right merely because doing it produces a better state of things than not doing it.

I am inclined to believe, though with some misgiving, that the word 'good' when applied to acts always means either 'right' or 'moral' (i.e. done because thought right by the agent) or virtuous (i.e. thought right but done from a kind of desire that usually leads to right acts), but that when applied to states or events, unless it mean useful, it always means either 'satisfying desire' or 'the sort of state or event which we should think it our duty in normal circumstances to bring about were it in our power'. Bacon seems to have recognized the distinction, though he misquoted Seneca, when he said: 'The good things which belong to prosperity are to be wished, but the good things that belong to adversity are to be admired.'[1]

We have already quoted Grote[2] as believing that an act may be judged right without being seen to lead to any state better than the state which its omission

[1] *Essays: Of Adversity.*

[2] See § 51 above.

would lead to. The same belief is strongly put by Ruskin :

'No man ever knows, or can know, what will be the ultimate result to himself, or to others, of any given line of conduct. But every man may know, and most of us do know, what is a just and unjust act. And all of us may know also, that the consequences of justice will be ultimately the best possible, both to others and ourselves, though we neither can say what *is* best, or how it is likely to come to pass.' [1]

In the second sentence I should be inclined to insert the word 'sometimes' before 'know', and in the last to substitute 'hope' or 'trust' for 'know'.

(65) The *Summum Bonum* has, I believe, been the *ignis fatuus* of moral philosophy. It is sometimes a blanket-term to cover everything which has any value, as when we say that a life perfect in righteousness and in the enjoyment of happiness, truth, and beauty would be The Good. This is the sense in which Kant speaks of the *summum bonum* or *bonum consummatum* as an externally effected union of duty with satisfaction, and in which Aristotle often speaks of *Εὐδαιμονία*. Sometimes it means what we ought to choose, or the good which most concerns us as moral creatures, and this is plainly morality, which alone is always obligatory and always in our power. This is the sense in which Aristotle also often speaks of *Εὐδαιμονία*, and in which Kant says that nothing has unconditional worth but the good will (*bonum supremum*). But to ask whether happiness or morality is '*the* good' conveys to me no clear meaning. If it mean 'which do we desire most?' the plain answer is that we all desire happiness, but that all of us some of the time and some of us all the time do

[1] *Unto This Last*, i.

not desire morality at all. If it mean 'which, when they are incompatible, ought we to choose?' the answer is equally plain. If it mean 'which is the purpose of our existence from the point of view of God?' I must reply that I do not know, and as a moral philosopher I do not care, though Kant's contention is convincing that if a wise Creator had intended us for happiness we should have been better equipped. But I shall refer to this question again in my last section.[1] A man desires many different things for their own sake, and we have shown the fallacy of trying to reduce all these desires to the desire for pleasure. He has also many different duties; and, though it is proper to ask whether there be any common quality which makes them his duties, we must not assume that this is so.

Note. If we have recognized that actions are not always right merely in proportion to the greatness of a good which they bring about, we see how it is that two men, engaged in thwarting each other's efforts, may both be acting not only morally but in fact rightly. It may be the duty of A and B each to do all that he honestly can to pay his debts and, for that purpose, to compete against the other for some post, which each is equally fit to occupy. Each might see the other's conduct to be right as well as moral (cf. § 61).

[1] § 103.

IX

DUTY FOR DUTY'S SAKE

(66) THERE next falls to be considered a great system of moral philosophy which attempts indeed, like those we have considered, to demonstrate the kinds of act that we ought to do, or at least those that we ought not to do, but deduces them from the idea of rightness or duty instead of from the idea of an end or good to be achieved. We noticed in the theory of the Common Good a continual uncertainty whether that which was a common good was the moral (or perhaps right) act itself or some 'common source of satisfaction' produced by it. The view we have now to deal with decides unequivocally for the first alternative.[1] It holds that the only absolutely or unconditionally good thing is morality, and the only moral act is one done solely because it is thought right, and not from interest in any end to be produced. There is no other end whose pursuit we do not in certain circumstances judge wrong; happiness, for myself, for another, for all. There is no interest whose satisfaction we may not sometimes judge wrong; self-love, friendship, love of family, patriotism. But however misguided a man may be, we never blame him for reverencing duty, that is, for trying to find out what is right to do and acting upon his conclusion. All other moral theories, it is held, have enslaved moral reason to desire, have made it *heteronomous*; for they have told us hypothetically that if or so far as we find that we desire happiness or anything else for ourselves or others

[1] This at least I take to be Kant's primary view. It is true that he afterwards inconsistently modifies it.

we shall do well to take certain means; whereas this theory makes the moral reason *autonomous*, legislative for itself, and states our obligation to obey it categorically. And just because moral obligation is asserted by reason categorically, and is not conditional on the possession of some desire, it is universal, applying not to me or to you but to every rational being.[1] It is the essence of law to be universal. So morality would *be* the 'common good' in the sense that it is the only thing impartially valued by, because equally binding on all. And it is of equal value in all its instances, so that every rational creature potentially has unconditional worth. Consequently so far as he 'realizes' this capacity for morality and 'sacrifices' his contrary desires, he has moral merit or worth, and it becomes the duty of others to make his purpose their own. So in a world where all men were moral we should find every individual respecting the morality, though not perhaps the wisdom, of all the others, and though there might still be opposition owing to error, there would be no enmity or suspicion, but a reign of universal love, which is essentially the Kingdom of Heaven.

(67) I have tried, so far, to represent the point of view in my own way, emphasizing the important truth which I think it contains and leaving the difficulties and ambiguities for future discussion. But it is a theory so necessarily identified with its greatest supporter, Kant, that it becomes necessary to turn to a closer criticism of the actual form which he gives it. In the account, even as given already, there are two ambiguities, which in Kant's own statement seem to me absolute errors. These two errors are closely connected. The first is

[1] Cf. § 10.

that he never clearly recognizes the most obvious distinction of the actual moral life, that between moral conduct and right conduct, between what the agent thinks to be right and what is right. The second is that he thinks that we can judge the rightness or wrongness of an act without considering the consequences in the way of satisfaction either to ourselves or to other persons.

(1) The first error is a curious one for Kant to have made. He emphatically states that the act is moral, not because it is the bringing about of this or that result, but only if it is done from respect for duty. The inevitable conclusion seems to be that a really right act, the one we really ought to do, may be done from nonmoral motives and therefore not be moral. And he, in fact, implies this. But he never seems to admit the corollary that a wrong act, one we really ought not to do, may be done from the moral motive that it is thought right, and therefore have full moral value. The failure to recognize a distinction so familiar in moral experience, and demanded by his own theory, surely points to some very significant prepossession of Kant's mind. An obvious explanation would be that every act thought right is thereby right. This is a view which we must consider later, but it was clearly not Kant's. Rightness is for him objective, nothing if not universally valid.

(2) He does not allow that the rightness of an act can be affected by its actual consequences nor its morality by the foreseen consequences. Accordingly for him there should never be any difficulty in judging correctly. What acts are right can be deduced immediately from the notion of rightness, somewhat as from the notion of a triangle we can immediately see that there can be only

three types of triangle, equilateral, scalene, and isosceles. Consequently an act that is honestly thought right is almost certainly right. As in mathematics, we may be ignorant, but we often clearly see a proof and then we can hardly be wrong.

The failure of Kant's attempt to deduce from the notion of duty a code of morals has been so often exposed that the task of insulting over it is ungracious, but it must be faced.

(68) Since the moral law, as being law, must not depend on any particular desires, but be universal and admit of no exceptions, we must ask ourselves whether the act we *propose to do* is one which we can *also* will without contradiction should become a universal law. If not it is wrong.

(1) First, we must notice that this test is merely negative. It does not pretend to suggest actions to us; otherwise any absurdity, such as to eat meat five times daily, would become a duty, if its universalization involved no contradiction. For the suggestion of action apparently we must go to desire; but Kant could hardly have meant this.

(2) Next we see that, if we ask whether we can will that a suggested act should be done by all men in precisely my circumstances, the answer is no guide at all. In exactly my circumstances, if they could ever be repeated, of course the act I ought to do ought to be done, and no contradiction could ever arise. If, on the other hand, we say nothing about similarity of circumstances, we are driven to such absurdities as saying that, if it would be self-contradictory for everybody to give three-fourths of his income to charity, it must be immoral for any millionaire to do so to-day; or that if

universal celibacy would be self-contradictory, Kant's was a crime. Kant's examples are:

(*a*) *Lying*. I can will to lie, but if everybody lied no one would be believed, and therefore the purpose of lying would be frustrated and nobody could effectively lie. This is the only example that pretends strictly to illustrate his principle. Its absurdity, whether as an example of how to test the wrongness of an act or of an explanation of why it is wrong to lie, is sufficiently obvious. And it does take account of consequences, for it assumes that my untrue statements will deceive. If it did not assume this, it would be still absurder, for it would put the novel on a level with forgery. Clearly stealing could be treated on the same lines as lying. But it is noteworthy that Kant has not attempted to apply them to assault. Battery remains painful, however common and expected. So even if all angry men hit out I could still hit out in anger effectively and without self-contradiction. Perhaps the best example for Kant would be the scruple I might feel to abstain from voting, however important the business I should have to neglect and however slight the chance of my vote affecting any political issue. This scruple depends on the thought that if all abstained, even in similar circumstances, the government could not be carried on. It is not altogether removed by the knowledge that most will vote whether I do or not. I may still feel that Gallios, though quite harmless, do not quite play the game. But in general the attempt to determine whether this is right conduct for me here and now, by considering the consequences of everybody acting in the same way always, is futile.

(*b*) *Suicide*. Kant might have said that if everybody killed himself there would be nobody left to kill. This would have been the parallel to the argument about lying; but, perhaps because he saw that this argument was ludicrous, he unexpectedly argues that to use an instinct—desire of happiness—implanted in us for self-preservation as a motive to self-destruction is contradictory. This kind of contradiction has nothing to do with universality; it arises in each particular case. And it assumes that nature's purpose was not to preserve the happy and successful, letting the others go hang themselves.

(*c*) *Idleness.* A man with good abilities but sufficient means may will to live a life of idleness, neglecting his faculties. But, according to Kant, he could not will that this law should be universally followed, since, as a reasonable being, he must will the development of human faculties. Here the proof by contradiction has simply slipped away. Kant admits that the world could carry on if such selfishness were universal. Only it would be no more right for others than for one.

(*d*) A man, though he refrain from injuring his neighbours, may decide not to go out of his way to help them. Again the human race could subsist if this were the general practice—perhaps, as Kant thinks, it would be better off than it is now—; but the man cannot will such conduct to be universal, for the situation might arise when he would need help himself. I do not suppose that Kant meant[1] that the man's selfishness would bring about either his own need or the refusal of others to relieve it, so the maxim is not one of mere prudence, but it is hard to see what other meaning it could have. It amounts to saying I must not do anything which I should not *like* others to do to me. This would forbid

[1] Cf. his *Preface to the Metaphysical Elements of Ethics.*

all punishment, and all acts which are unpleasant to anybody.

Kant admits that these last two instances do not strictly produce any contradictions. Some acts, he says, cannot even be *conceived* as universalized without contradiction, and our obligation to avoid them is strict and perfect. Of others we can only say that they cannot be *willed* to be universalized without 'contradiction of the will'. This can hardly mean that I cannot *want* all men, including myself, to behave in this way. A weak man could not want all, including himself, to abstain from helping neighbours; but a strong man could, if their abstention was the price of his. The only other meaning that I can suggest is that a man in acting selfishly recognizes, especially if he ask himself what he would think of others doing the like, that it is wrong. Kant thinks our obligation to avoid these last two classes[1] of acts less strict or perfect than the obligation not to lie, steal, or commit suicide.

On these lines we must say that Kant fails to give us a complete guide to the actions we should avoid—not to speak of those we should do—and indeed to give any reason for avoiding any actions, even lies, which convinces anybody inclined to think them right.

(69) Probably because he was himself dissatisfied with this proof, Kant adds a second, which he declares to be another form of the first, though it really appears to be inconsistent with it, since it demands that our action should aim at certain results.

The argument is that, as morality is the only unconditionally good thing, we must treat all rational beings, since they are capable of morality, as ends, and

[1] (*c*) and (*d*) above.

never as means only. This is very obscure. It might mean:—

(*a*) That we should promote their morality. But on Kant's view of morality this is impossible.[1] We could only remove temptation or add inducement, which would not affect their self-determined obedience to moral law.

(*b*) That we should satisfy their desires and so make them happy. This is what Kant explicitly and repeatedly says he does mean. But it is quite inconsistent with his general position and with the facts. It pays regard to consequences, it gives a value to desires of rational beings, and it does not distinguish between the qualities of those desires or of their satisfactions.

(*c*) The most consistent meaning we could suggest, though Kant himself gives only a vague hint of it, is that so far as men realize their moral capacities (that is, do what they think right), we should aid them in achieving a successful issue to their moral acts. For instance, if, out of respect for duty, they make sacrifices to educate their children, we should see that their children get a good education. Even this allows a regard for consequences. In the sort of act which Kant regards as most strictly moral, such as telling the truth when it leads to crime and suffering, it is hard to see the duty or possibility of 'making the ends of the moral agent our own'. For his morality consists in paying no attention to ends. The results of his act are bad. And further if men in doing what they think right do what we think wrong, it is hard to think it can be our duty to 'make their ends our own'. Ought we then to say that we should promote the success of those efforts which all or

[1] *Preface to the Metaphysical Elements of Ethics*, iv.

most men think right? Kant does seem to hint at something of this kind when he describes his ideal Kingdom of Ends as a system of all rational beings each treating as ends in themselves all the others, together with the ends that they may set themselves, but 'with abstraction from the difference of persons and the content of their private ends'. I do not see how this would be done. It is as obscure as Rousseau's General Will, which is always right because the private selfishnesses cancel out.

(70) The point of what may seem a stale and unprofitable criticism of Kant's arguments is to show that it is as impossible to deduce any code of duties from the notion of duty as it is from the notion of a good or end. Kant was right in his recognition of this latter impossibility, wrong in his failure to see the former. The most usual criticism brought against his theory of morality is that it is 'purely formal'. If by this be meant that, while correctly analysing the notion of morality and obligation, he fails to give us a code of the acts to which we are morally obliged, the statement is true. But I venture to think that moral philosophy should be in that sense formal; it should define morality, distinguishing it from right conduct and from other things with which it has been confused; it should not try to play the part of that conscience or moral reason which acts primarily upon particular situations and whose immediate judgements neither need nor can be demonstrated.

(71) But there is another sense in which the charge of formality has more importance. If Kant was mistaken in thinking that analysis of the notion of duty would produce rules of right conduct, if the universal

conception of duty does not generate its own applications, how, it may well be asked, does it ever get applied? Provisionally I should be content to answer: In the same way that the universal notions of truth and beauty get applied. Particular truths of science or history are not discovered by reflecting on the nature of truth. We do not apprehend the beauty of a picture or poem by a process of deduction from the idea of beauty. We should not reach the distinctions of right and wrong, of true and false, of beautiful and ugly, by mere experience of a world we share with the animals unless our mind were so constituted as to recognize them, but it is in particular instances that we first do so. It is a necessary part of the nature of a rational being to view acts under the notions of right and wrong. Like the animals we are moved by desire. Unlike them, probably, we are able to reflect upon the incompatibility of our desires among themselves and with those of other persons. And, instead of being the prey of that desire which is at any moment strongest, we pass a judgement upon the rightness of satisfying this or that desire of our own, or this or that desire of others which we can imagine through sympathy. Kant perhaps precluded himself from this account by his hedonistic error in thinking that all desires were desires for pleasure. All desires were therefore really the same desire, and it would be hard to see how the satisfaction of one would be more right than that of another. All that could be said would be what he did say, that a good man's desire of happiness should be gratified rather than a bad man's. He failed to see that the existence of desires in the world is the presupposition of there being not only any merit (in resisting our own) but any duty (to satisfy other people's). For duty, or at least our duty to others, consists in the right or due distribution of satisfactions and perhaps dissatisfactions. I may find in myself as in others a desire which in certain circumstances I think I ought to satisfy, but if I or they had not had that desire no reflection on an abstract idea of duty would ever have suggested the action to me. I am doubtful if there can be a duty whose execution will not bring some satisfaction to somebody. It might even plausibly be said that I never judge an act to be my duty until I have discovered in myself some interest, however slight, in its performance. For, as Hume pointed out, we are so constituted as to sympathize with all satisfactions of others; though, as he failed consistently to recognize, this sympathy, which we generally approve, and think it right to act on, is commonly weaker than selfish or malevolent desires which we generally condemn. The difficulties of these views we must consider later.

If Kant be interpreted, not without some excuse, as meaning that acts done out of reverence for the moral law, that is because they are thought right, are thereby right, his doctrine would be indeed 'formal' and 'empty'. For how could we think anything really right if we also thought its rightness dependent on our recognition?

X

IDIOPSYCHOLOGICAL ETHICS

(72) I DO not know any commonly accepted name for the view which I am about to consider, and have therefore adopted the curious title invented, with many apologies, by its chief exponent James Martineau, in his *Types of Ethical Theory*.[1]

By calling his system psychological he merely means that he starts from the facts of consciousness and not from any theory as to the nature of the universe. By calling it idiopsychological he means that he 'starts from the postulates of the moral consciousness as they are',[2] taking them as ultimate and irreducible to unmoral sources. But Martineau's own view is by no means the only one which has a right to the name idiopsychological thus defined, did others care to dispute it. What I now propose to discuss is really the view that the rightness of an act depends upon the motive from which it was done.

(73) Martineau, I think, starts from Kant's discovery that only the good will has moral value and that actual consequences and everything but motive are irrelevant to moral worth. He also shares Kant's failure to distinguish clearly moral action, or action which is done because it is thought right, from action which really is right; and, feeling embarrassed by the unacknowledged ambiguity between the two, cuts the knot by declaring that moral action and right action are the same. In other words, there is in no situation an absolutely right action, but an action is right relatively to alternative

[1] See Bibliography. [2] Vol. i, p. xxvii (2nd edition).

actions if it springs from a higher motive. For this reason the good man both does and approves it. It is always the motive or spring of action which we judge, and we judge it by comparing it, as higher or lower, with others. 'The instant that any contending principles press their invitations on (a man), *there*, too, is the consciousness of their respective rights; and if he is betrayed into wrong, he is self-betrayed. His *duty* consists in acting *from the right affection*, about which he is never left in doubt; it is his *wisdom* only that consists in *pursuing the right end*.' [1] 'In our consciousness, the only positive forces are the living springs of activity which, in and by themselves, are neither morally evil nor morally good, but which, having a relative worth *inter se*, present a moral quality for the exercise of our preference upon them. It is quite possible that an impulse may become the object of our preference simply on account of its superior worth, independent of any isolated urgency of its own; and thus moral good is capable of becoming a positive energy determining into existence what else would not appear.' [2] Yet the function of conscience is 'purely judicial'.[3] 'To find the *motive* you must go to the impulses on which the conscience pronounces: to find the determining agent you must go to the subsequent will. The act is carried out by the energy of its own spring, just as much as if there had been no competitor and no pause; and to this the external observer would unhesitatingly refer as its motive. There is, however, besides, hidden perhaps from the bystander, the prior internal act of choice

[1] Vol. ii, p. 72. By *right* affection Martineau must here mean 'best affection present'. What he means by *right end* I do not know. [2] p. 89. [3] p. 186.

between the possibilities present and now judged; and if it select the better, this is certainly an example of the mind's preference for the good, and may, in an intelligible sense, be referred to the *love of right* or *of virtue*.'[1]

Two questions, he says, have to be clearly distinguished: 'What, in point of motive, is right relatively to the agent in his given position?' and 'What, in point of social effect, is the right mode of action to be instituted under the supposed conditions?' 'With (the first) alone we have here to do: the other belongs to objective ethics, which have to select the reasonable action for carrying out the moral motive.' Consequently the cruelty of the convinced inquisitor is 'wrong, not in its principle but in its application; because it is a blunder, not because it is a sin'.[2]

As a formal and exact definition of right we are told, 'Every action is RIGHT, which, in presence of a lower principle, follows a higher'.[3] And, comparing this with our first quotation, we see the attempt to obliterate the distinction of right and moral: a man cannot be mistaken in the relative worth of his impulses, and to follow the higher is always right.

(74) Here, however, the difficulties begin. It has to be acknowledged that the judgement on the relative worth of an impulse is, at least in the first instance, always passed upon a particular occurrence of that impulse in contrast with some other.[4] And in order to compare the worth of impulses which arise in us on a particular occasion, we have to consider the worth of the objects to which each is directed: 'Its value is, *per se*, indeterminate.'[5] 'Fears cannot be appraised without

[1] p. 227. [2] pp. 232–4. [3] p. 270.
[4] pp. 48–52. [5] p. 198.

reference to the worth of the objects feared; just as Hope rises to the noble or sinks to the base, and Love may be a grace or a degradation, according to the object that fixes the eye or wins the heart.' Further, in comparing the worth of an impulse of pity with one of parental affection, we are allowed to consider questions such as whether the gratification of the latter may not be postponed more safely than that of the former, for which an opportunity may not recur. This seems to mean that the impulse to relieve a stranger's urgent need is to be rated higher than one to get an educational advantage for my child, if I can do the latter next year; or, in Martineau's own words, though with my italics, if I do nothing 'inconsistent with the permanent *obligation* to the child'.[1] A similar inconsistency arises in dealing with justice.[2] It is clear that in fact the worth of an impulse is only to be estimated by the 'worth' (i.e. rightness) of the act it here and now impels me to do, and that nothing in the situation or consequences need be irrelevant to that estimation.

The essential difference of a doctrine like Butler's or Martineau's from Kant's is that it allows to reason or conscience a merely judicial function of deciding between litigants who appeal to it, but not of suggesting any act of its own motion. Some difficulties for such a view will be discussed under the topics of Rights and Punishment. Meanwhile we need only notice that the distinction between a right act and a moral act, which the doctrine seemed designed to avoid, is not avoided.

(75) If we cannot ourselves clear up these difficulties we should at least try to state them as clearly as we can. A rational being finds himself in a situation in

[1] pp. 220–1. [2] pp. 246–54. Cf. p. 275.

which there is some act that he thinks he ought to do (and which therefore he must think he can do). If he does it for this reason, that is a moral act. But he may be mistaken in thinking that he ought to do this act; it may be that he ought to have done some other, and this we should naturally call the right act or the absolutely right act. So in his error he acted morally but not rightly. There is, therefore, a right act (which must be a possible act) which may not be known to be right. Now the rightness of an act depends partly upon the situation, that is upon the existing relation of the parties (in the way of contract or other kind of obligation), and partly upon the way in which the act affects the development of that situation. Among those circumstances composing the situation which may well be relevant to the rightness of the act will be my own character and capacities and those of the people I am dealing with; for instance, in accepting or appointing to an office. Also the opinions and beliefs of people must be considered; what I might properly say to one person would violate the religious sensibilities or the modesty of another. It is now clear that not only may I be ignorant of some of the conditions relevant to the rightness of my act, but that I must be; or at least that I can never know that I am not. For neither can I certainly know all the relevant history, opinions, beliefs, and feelings of those concerned and their and my capacities, nor can I know how I am affecting the development of that situation. The consequences of every act are infinite, and the remoter are as relevant to its absolute rightness as the nearer. If the activities of a charity affect the rightness of drawing a cheque, so do the consequences of these activities all over the world to the end of human history; but these I know I cannot know. The absolutely right act, then, for a man to do is impossible for him to know and therefore impossible for him to do except by accident. Now we originally said that the right act in a situation must be a possible act in the situation, but if it is not possible (or at least not discoverable) but is only the act which would be right if it were possible, we are left with an ideal in a vacuum.

If, then, it be impossible for me to be sure what is the absolutely right act it cannot be my duty to do it. We can only say that it is my duty to try to do it.

It may be objected to all this that it is improper to count my knowledge or ignorance or opinion about the situation in which I am acting as part of that situation. Certainly these would not affect the absolutely right act, if that mean the act an omniscient being ought to do. But as I am not omniscient and know I am not omniscient it can hardly be my duty to act as if I were: that would imply that I ought not to try to learn about the situation and consequences.

If we neglect the blemish of our ignorance and say it is our duty to do the absolutely right act, we may as well neglect every blemish in the situation and ask, What would be our duties in a world where not only were we omniscient but everybody perfectly and inexpugnably good and happy? The answer is there would be none.

The absolute rightness of an act, then, may depend on conditions, past, present, and future, which I know I cannot know. But since this ignorance of some of the conditions is an element of the situation in which I have to act, and since it is always the situation which determines the rightness of an act, there ought to be an act right for me to do in my partial ignorance. There must be an act I ought to do with such knowledge of the circumstances as I have. This, for lack of a better name, I propose to call 'the act right for me'. But doing this need not be identical with doing a moral act, for that is the act I *think* I ought to do with such knowledge of the circumstances as I have; and in that thinking I may be mistaken. Some moralists, as we have seen, seem to suppose that, assuming the situation and consequences to be what we think them, it is impossible to judge wrongly of an act's rightness. But we have also seen that this leads to serious paradox. Yet if it be possible to misjudge morally (all the facts being assumed), the mistake may be one which I cannot now help (even if sometimes I might have prevented it by training myself better in the past). Consequently I cannot now know the right act for me any more than the absolutely right act, and therefore I cannot do it except by accident. I myself hold that it is sometimes possible to *know* that an act is right for me, or for any one in the same circumstances and with the same knowledge of them. If I do it for that reason, then, the moral act is the 'act right for me'.

There appear, then, in any situation to be three acts, possibly all different or by chance coinciding, to each of which some kind of approval, commendation, or assent would be given. First, there is the absolutely right act, the right act for an omniscient being; second, there is the right act for me, the one which is really the duty of a being with my knowledge of the facts; and, last, the act I think right, which is moral if done for that reason (if I know it to be right[1] the last two coincide). Further, we give an additional approval to the doing of a moral

[1] Right for me, i.e. if the circumstances are what I think.

act in proportion to the strength of the desire not to do it or to do something inconsistent with it. This is the attribution of moral desert. To which of those three is properly applicable the phrase 'the act I ought to do' or 'my duty'? Not apparently to either of the two first; for when I cannot know them I cannot do them except by accident. Yet to apply these phrases to the third and say that the act I think right is my duty and the act I ought to do seems equivalent to saying that what I think right for me to do always is right for me to do and that what I think to be my duty is my duty: which seems to be plain nonsense. If it were true, any opinion as to my duty would be as good as any other, and to say, as we must, that it is often our duty to try to find out more fully what our other duties are would be absurd. I suppose we may conclude that I ought to try to do what is absolutely right, since I might by luck succeed and the harder I try the better the chances; I am less unlikely to succeed in doing what is right for me; I am quite able to make these attempts; and that is moral. My duty is to be moral, and that is to try to do what is right. The difficulties discussed in this section, then, though real difficulties for the correct description of morality, throw no doubt whatever on the validity of moral obligation. Rather the careless or sophistic neglect of such distinctions may result in ambiguous language which is apt to have that effect.

XI
RIGHTS

(76) Kant could find no materials for the filling in of his empty form that the right action consists in obedience to the moral law. Failing to make any headway by juggling with the notion of contradiction, he fell back upon precisely the utilitarianism which it is his distinction to have condemned, and inconsistently suggested that we should make other rational beings happy. The difficulties in that have been discussed. We do not feel it equally our duty to seek all kinds of happiness for all people. We have, as Butler said, 'particular obligations'. In certain situations we can recognize certain actions as morally suitable, as obligatory for us to perform. We certainly speak of Rights; what we mean is obscure. Jurists have their definition of legal rights; so far as they speak of other rights they are confusing. Austin, in his *Lectures on Jurisprudence*, says: 'Strictly speaking, there are no rights but those which are the creatures of law; and I speak of any other kind of rights only in order that I may conform to the received language, which certainly does allow us to speak of moral rights not sanctioned by law; thus, for example, we speak of rights created by treaty.' [1]

Rights, other than legal, he divides into moral and divine, adding that all three kinds are 'necessarily acquired . . . through the might or power of another'.

Moral rights he defines in a sense in which I doubt whether the term be ever used. He says they are those 'conferred . . . by the opinion of the community

[1] xii, p. 354.

at large', and he seems to think they are so conferred 'so far as the members of (the) . . . community are severally constrained . . . by the opinion of the community'.[1]

Of the third kind he says: 'Every Divine right springs from the Divine law; and to the Divine law general utility is the index.' 'An act which a sovereign government (who can of course have no legal rights) has a Divine right to do, it, emphatically, has a right to do: if it had not a Divine right, it, emphatically, has not a right. An act which were generally useful the Divine law, as known through the principle of utility, has conferred on the sovereign government the right to do: an act which were generally pernicious the Divine law, as known through the same exponent, has not conferred on the sovereign government a right to do.' 'An act which conforms to the Divine law is styled, emphatically, just: an act which does not, is styled, emphatically, unjust.'[2] This class of divine rights or acts of justice corresponds to what I, and I fancy most people, call moral rights; except that I do not think that the only rights, any more than the only duties, are that the greatest happiness of the greatest number should be brought about. I do not think that utility is justice. So far as I can see, Austin's only reason for ascribing these rights to the law of God is that he believes that they are rights and has arbitrarily defined rights as acquired through the power of another and as being the creatures of law. Consequently he is bound to argue that nobody can recognize these rights unless he believe in a God whose purpose is the happiness of mankind. And in this he is clearly wrong. Perhaps

[1] vi, pp. 292–5. [2] vi, pp. 292–5.

for these reasons Holland in his *Elements of Jurisprudence* drops the divine rights and retains only Austin's legal and moral rights. Perhaps also because he saw that it is inaccurate to speak of the opinion of the community as constraining us (since what constrains us in this sense is our own opinion that the opinion of the community is likely to issue in overt acts) he alters the definition of a man's moral rights: 'If, irrespectively of having or not having this might' (to carry out his wishes, either by his own acts, or by influencing the acts of others), 'public opinion would view with approval, or at least with acquiescence, his so carrying out his wishes, and with disapproval any resistance made to his so doing; then he has a "moral right" so to carry out his wishes.'[1] But surely, in ordinary language, when we disapprove any resistance to a man's carrying out his wishes, we should say that this was *because* he had a right to do so, and should not think that we or anybody conferred the right by approval. General assent is as fallible a test of rights as of duties.

(77) For some reason, which I do not know, there is a greater tendency to identify rights with legal rights than duties with legal duties. Yet it would be a strange paradox that a man's rights are precisely what the laws of his country, however bad, allow him. We constantly criticize particular laws, such as a franchise, on the ground that they do not recognize some rights, and we speak of the rights of parents to obedience, the rights of weak nations, the right to have a verbal promise kept, when there is no law. When we speak of safeguarding the rights of minorities I suppose we mean that, if we knew how, we ought to make into legal rights those

[1] vii.

which already exist but are not yet 'recognized' either by law or by the opinion of the majority.

Consequently people have spoken of Natural Rights, generally meaning rights independent of legal sanction, rights which every man has as a man, and some at least of which most laws do and all laws should sanction. With the origin of this conception from the Roman *Ius Gentium* and *Ius Naturae* or from Greek international maritime law we are not concerned. The difficulty is to find anything to which a man, simply as a man, has a universal and indefeasible right. So, in opposition to this idea, a modification of the legal view has been put forward. Rights are no longer confined to claims recognized by law, but to those recognized in some vaguer way by the society to which the parties belong. Only as a member of a society, it is said, can one have a right, and only as a member of a society which recognizes a common good. To begin with, it is surely a strange phrase which suggests that a right or anything else comes into being by being *recognized*. All that can be meant is that among all the things which I ought to be given I have a *right* only to those which my society recognizes I ought to be given. If this were true I could have no disputed rights. What is meant by *my* society is obscure. Sometimes apparently it is the organized state to which I belong or in which I am residing: the objections to this are similar to those urged against the identification of rights with legal rights. Sometimes, apparently, it is any person or persons with whom I may find myself in relation, such as the stranger whom I meet upon a desert island, between whom and myself there would certainly seem to be rights—as for a fair distribution of water, labour, and the like. Clearly rights only *arise* in society (if that mean not in solitude); but it is hard to see how my right to a drink upon a desert island is diminished by a drunken sailor's inability to recognize it.

(78) What, then, is meant by the second condition: that rights only arise in societies which recognize a common good? We have seen that a common good may mean either (1) some act which all members of a group agree in thinking ought to be done, or (2) something from whose use they all may derive satisfaction, or (3) some state of things which they all desire should be brought about. In the first sense we should be told that all members of a group (or those advantaged thereby) have a right to have all and only those actions done which they all think ought to be done. This has the difficulties already pointed out. And further it would involve the denial of any rights on the part of lunatics, children, or animals, who cannot recognize duties, and so cannot be members of a group all of whose members do. In the second sense I should have a right to all and only those things (or all members of the group would have the right that I should have those things) which it is for the advantage of all or most members of the group I should possess—if they all know it and if it be possible for me to be given them. But, as already argued, it is difficult to see that a *just* distribution (that to which each party has a right) always results either in the greatest sum of satisfaction upon the whole or in any advantage at all to some party. In the third sense all members of a group would have the right that all and only those states of things should be brought about which all desire. But in this sense nobody could have a right contrary to anybody's desire. In none of these

three senses is it clear why the group considered should be smaller than the whole company of rational persons, posterity included. The doctrine of natural rights has been a justifiable protest against the suggestion that all rights are something conventional, dependent upon legislation, covenant, or general agreement. So far, it might properly have asserted that all rights, if they really are rights, are natural; a man has a 'natural' right that a compact, once entered into, should be kept. But usually a distinction has been drawn between natural and other rights, natural rights being those which hold for all men always, while other rights only arise in particular situations, perhaps in situations voluntarily created by one or both parties. But no right, not even that to life, is absolute so as to preclude all consideration of circumstances. So the distinction would seem to be in frequency and degree of obligation rather than in kind.

(79) It is commonly said that rights and duties are correlative, but two meanings are given to the statement. (*a*) It may mean that if anybody has a duty to do anything somebody has a right to have that thing done and vice versa, or (*b*) that everybody capable of rights must be capable of duties and vice versa.

(*a*) The only objection to the first interpretation is that it is my duty to be generous (in the sense of giving free gifts), but that nobody has a right to generosity; to which it might be replied that the term duty is not applicable, or not in the same sense, to generosity as it is to justice: where it strictly is my duty it is really the other party's right.

(*b*) The second interpretation implies that it is incorrect to speak of the rights of animals, children, or lunatics, though if children grow up or lunatics be cured they may become capable of rights. Posterity might still have rights that we should do certain things for it on the ground that though it will not have duties to us, yet it will have duties.

Clearly the real point of interest is to decide whether such a distinction of kind can be drawn among right acts that some would be called acts of duty or of obligation or satisfaction of rights, while others, such as acts of charity, would not. Many who maintain the distinction between justice and generosity, equating the former with the satisfaction of rights, would use the word duty of both; but it seems more natural language to make my duties conterminous with the rights of others, and to allow that if there be any right acts for me to do to which nobody has a right they are not my duties. It would still be undecided whether the existence of a right implies a corresponding duty only in some particular person, for instance a debtor, or whether it creates a secondary duty in all men to assist in securing its satisfaction.

(80) If we are to distinguish, among the admittedly right acts which I can do, a class called duties, to the performance of which other persons have rights, we ought to be able to state the *differentia*. This could not be that the class is that of acts legally enjoined or enforcible, nor yet of those to which I have committed myself by contract. It is sometimes suggested that men have a right not to be interfered with (except to prevent their interference with others), but no right to be helped; or that they have a right to liberty. I find it difficult to maintain the distinction of positive interference and negative neglect. I feel the same kind of obligation

(though less) to help a man out of a hole as not to shoulder him callously into it; to assist him in escaping from wrongful imprisonment or economic slavery as not to oppress him; and if parents and children have reciprocal rights, these are rights rather to benefits than to mere freedom.

(81) Some have accordingly denied the existence of any distinction in kind among right acts and reduced it to a difference in degree of obligation, explaining the common belief in such a distinction of kind by a cause similar to the reason offered for the distinction by those who allege it. They assert that there is both a duty and a right to civility or generosity, as there is to the payment of debts; usually a less stringent one; but sometimes my obligation would be to perform an act of so-called generosity rather than one of so-called justice, if they were incompatible. If I had only money to pay my wealthy creditor it might sometimes be my duty rather to succour a needy stranger. When asked to explain the current distinction of justice from generosity they make some such answer as the following. Among acts which are right and, speaking generally, even equally obligatory, it may be right to get some enforced by law, others not by law but by public opinion, and others not at all. Examples would be: of the first class, debts; of the second, charity in some proportion to means; of the third, presents to friends. The secure expectation of one's assets is so important that we have thought it right, so to speak, to socialize the obligation of debt-paying even at the loss of spontaneity in the debtor. The value of present-giving and receiving depends so much upon spontaneity and even unexpectedness, that to leave it to private initiative seems right. The relief of

distress falls between the two; more of it is left to private initiative in some times and countries than in others. When a class of action has been enjoined by law this gives an additional obligation to those instances of it which would be right in any event, and some prima facie obligation to those which would not, unless by themselves they would be very wrong. The same may be said less certainly of acts which are expected of us because they fall into a class enjoined by public opinion. Both kinds of act may be expected of any man without expecting him to be exceptionally enlightened. Those whose view I am describing should, I think, consistently say that our friends have an unclaimable right to the presents which it is proper for us to give them; charities have a right, claimable but not enforceable, to my reasonable subscription; creditors have an enforceable right to their debts.

Another reason, besides that suggested, why some right acts ought to be claimed, or even enforced, but not others, is that the person who should do and the persons who should receive a benefit that ought to be conferred may be very variously clear or doubtful. To whom I should pay my debts is usually clear; to which charities, of all the useful ones, I should subscribe, is to be decided by proximity or by tossing up. Somebody, on the other hand, ought to help any good charity, but it is hard to determine who. Perhaps it might be said that it is the community which has the right that certain of its individual members should be helped; but it is not easy to say that a community ought *in the person of some of its members* to help. Such expressions seem artificial, and the need for them throws suspicion on the theory they are meant to support.

(82) Against this view that our rights are only those important classes of action which in a great majority of cases it is right for people to do to us, it is no objection that it is sometimes right for me to give people that to which they have no right. That has been allowed for in the view.[1] It is more serious to allege that I sometimes ought not to enforce my admitted right. For it may be urged that, on the view which we are considering, this would be to say that it is not right for me to take what it is right for others to give me. But the difficulty, such as it is, is of wider extent. Just as creditors ought sometimes to remit what debtors ought to pay if it were not remitted, so I often ought to give what nobody ought to take from me by force; and so, either of two brothers perhaps ought to sacrifice his life to save the other: either ought to give what neither ought by force to *take*, or even to demand.

(83) I am inclined to say that in some situations of obligation to another person I find open to me an indefinite number of actions which can be graded on a scale of the amount of satisfaction that they will give him; and that somewhere on that scale I draw a more or less distinct line and say that, if my action falls below it, I fail to satisfy the other party's right, while, if it rises above it, I do for him more than his right. In some situations it seems possible to draw this line with tolerable clearness, in others not, but perhaps we are always inclined to look for it and yet never able to make

[1] By the suggestion that among the acts that I ought to do to a man he is only said to have a right to those which he ought for various reasons to claim. The obvious criticism is that the reason he ought to claim them has not really been shown to be anything except that he has a right.

it quite distinct. For instance, I owe something in the way of obedience and attention to my parents: how much on any given occasion may be determined by my other duties; but if these do not conflict with my duty to them, it would be hard to define its limits. It is worth noticing that, in ordinary, as distinct from legal, language, what a man 'has no right to' usually means what other persons have a right to and what, therefore, he ought not to have. Or again, if I have promised to 'do my utmost' for a man or to pay him 'as soon as I possibly can', he evidently has some right that I should make sacrifices of my own interests, and even of those interests of others which it would be right for me to satisfy had I not so promised. But just how far he has a right that I should go in this direction cannot be said in general, and wherever we fix the line it will be right for me to go beyond it and, so long as I do not injure others, to do him rather more than 'bare justice'. I cannot be 'generous' to him till I have been 'just', so the obligation to be 'just' is greater and therefore prior, yet it does not decrease with a bound at one point, but by imperceptible gradations. If, on the other hand, I have promised him a fixed sum on a fixed date his right seems clear, but disputes may always arise about the letter and the spirit of the obligation; I may be vexatious or I may give good measure pressed down and running over.

(84) There is clearly a connexion, though not a coincidence, between rights and legal rights, and since laws are all general, I suspect that the distinction between what a man has a right to and what it is right for me to give him depends upon the difficulty of applying general rules of conduct to particular cases. If we

believe in absolute rights, and say in general that a man has always a right to have a promise kept and always a right to life, we may some day find that we cannot keep a promise without endangering a life or breaking another promise. The question then arises which 'right' I ought to satisfy, and it becomes clear that, after all, 'rights' ought not always to be satisfied, since they cannot be, either because it is physically impossible or because one is incompatible with another. But I find it impossible to say that a man has a right to what he cannot have. Those who believe in indefeasible rights and correlative absolute obligations are driven to the strange paradox that in order to do my paramount duty I may have to leave others, which are still duties, undone; and consequently I must feel remorse for doing my paramount duty, though no doubt less than if I had done some other duty; and they should add that I must give some blame and punishment to a man who in order to do his paramount duty has to leave others undone. But these duties which cannot be done if I fulfil my paramount duty are really only hypothetical duties, which I ought to have fulfilled in other circumstances. They get called duties by an empirical generalization because generally, perhaps ninety-nine times out of a hundred, we have judged it our duty to keep our promise or to obey our parents or the law.[1] And the same I believe to be true, if less obvious, about rights. For, if it be urged that we say *ceteris paribus* the first applicant should be given the post and that nobody would say this *ceteris paribus* about the last, this only means that I have often felt an obligation to give a post to the first applicant—that priority has on those occasions

[1] Cf. Ch. XIII, especially § 91.

constituted a right. And I must remember also that *ceteris paribus* it should be given to the fittest applicant, and also to the most deserving and to the neediest, and also to a fellow countryman, or perhaps to my friend or my enemy. The only claim to the post which must be satisfied, without some such qualification as *ceteris paribus*, is the claim of the man who in this instance ought to be given it.

XII
PUNISHMENT

(85) We have been led to think of a right as that which in certain circumstances is *due* to one man from another. But hitherto we have only considered satisfactions as being due. Can something be due to a man which he does not desire and which will not satisfy him when he has got it? Can pain be due to him: has he ever a right to punishment? The various schools of utilitarians have answered or evaded the question by putting the whole duty of punishment into prevention, so that it is not the author of a crime but others who have a right that he should be punished, in order to protect them from like troubles in the future. Pain, they say, is an evil, and its infliction can only be justified as a means to a greater amount of pleasure. We should therefore hang a man, guilty or not guilty, if we think the example likely to prevent two or more murders. We may and should give a man as many strokes of the cat as we think a good felicific investment, remembering, however, that here too there is perhaps a law of diminishing returns. To give him twenty-five, if that is no more intimidating than twenty-four, or if an additional five would have prevented crimes causing ten strokes' worth of pain, is wrong. There is, however, a slight complication. Whether we like it or not, there are desires for vengeance on the part of the criminal's victims and of those who sympathize with them; and the pleasure felt in the satisfaction of these desires, and even by a few abnormal persons in the infliction of pain as such, must be entered in our balance, just as on the other side we

must enter the pain of a few sensitive people on hearing of the punishment. This clearly seems to the ordinary man a very artificial account of punishment, which appears at first sight to be thus put into the same category as quarantine, where also we inflict inconvenience for the good of others. It may be objected that the purpose of quarantine is not to terrify other people out of catching small-pox, and that therefore we make it as pleasant as may be. But it would still appear that, if prevention of crime be the whole justification and nature of punishment, then the hanging of an innocent man who is universally believed guilty is as ideal an instance of punishment as can be conceived. To plead that he had not deserved it would be to introduce the retribution theory.

(86) More fashionable at the moment is the reformatory view. And not only was and is the amendment of legal punishment in this direction an urgent duty, but philosophically it is less erroneous to put the essence of punishment in reform than in deterrence. But it also is erroneous. If punishment were simply the effort to improve a man it would be indistinguishable from education, which is most often both compulsory and painful. It will hardly be questioned that, when we punish a man by imprisonment, we should at the same time educate him, if he still be capable of it, technically and intellectually, as well as morally. But if the education were pleasanter and more profitable than his ordinary avocations we should not be punishing him. Surely we must consider the nature of punishment and that of reward together; only the fact that rewards are not so highly organized by the state has obscured this propriety. A man who felt it incumbent on him to

reward faithful service with a pension would be offended at the suggestion that this was no proper reward unless he published it in the newspapers so as to encourage others, or that the recipient himself was too old for encouragement. He would say that the reward was *deserved*. And the same must be said of punishment. To deny the retributive element in punishment is to deny any meaning to the words desert, merit, justice, and, I think, forgiveness.

(87) The word forgiveness is ambiguous: it may mean putting away personal animosity, and in this sense it is, as Christianity teaches, always a duty. We should try to feel to those who injure us as to those who injure others. But generally it means the remission of a due punishment, and, if punishment were exemplary alone, this would always be wrong. If punishment were solely retributive we ought always to remit it when the offender has repented, could we be sure of his genuine repentance. For remorse is the penalty that fits the crime, that which all punishment seeks to simulate and to stimulate. But it is seldom possible to prove repentance, though voluntary confession and restitution are good evidence. Repentance is more than recognizing that the act was wrong: the agent did that at the time of acting, or there would be nothing to repent of. It may be urged that if the analogy of reward to punishment were complete, and if punishment ought to be remitted when repentance is ascertained, then reward ought to be cancelled when we are satisfied that the meritorious man's conscience warmly approves him; for this is virtue's own reward. I suppose we ought by reward both to express our sympathy with a man's own self-approval and also to stimulate it if it be deficient;

but if his conscience really smite him we ought perhaps to express sympathy with him as smitten rather than as smiter. Another difference is that punishment should not be inflicted by the injured party, but a reward may be given by the original beneficiary.

(88) It is often objected to retribution that it is only a development of vengeance. The truth is that in almost the most elementary human vengeance there are obscure premonitions of the moral notion of punishment. Hardly any savage but in vengeance persuades himself he has been wronged; he feels differently towards the man who falls against him and the man who hits him. The prejudice against recognizing the retributive element in punishment has arisen, I think, from a too bare identification of punishment with pain and even with the *lex talionis*. Retribution is not an eye for an eye. It would be no more possible or appropriate for a parent to punish his children's disobedience by disobeying them than for the child to reward its mother's devotion by feeding her or educating her. Nor is retribution the mere occurrence of pain. A murderer is not punished by the pain of having cancer, but only by a pain which is given him, and which he knows is given him, because of his guilt. The essential thing in punishment, then, is not pain but the expression of censure, which is necessarily painful and tries to approximate to the ideal pain of remorse. Hence punishment has its best chance of reforming when it is recognized as being given retributively, that is, because it is deserved. From Plato [1] downwards it has been objected to retribution that pain added to guilt is the addition of evil to evil. But it seems self-evident that guilt with

[1] *Republic* 335, 380.

its appropriate pain of remorse is something that ought if possible to be substituted for guilt complacent and insulting. We cannot put remorse ready-made into a criminal's mind, but we can stimulate it by giving him a pain akin to that of remorse, making him feel the indignation of impartial observers. For though neither our intellectual nor our moral growth is merely imitative, both develop by the stimulus of seeing ourselves in the mirror of other minds.

(89) It is sometimes argued against the retributive theory of punishment, that even if a certain amount of guilt did deserve a certain amount of pain it would be impossible to say how much, and that yet to exceed that amount would be an outrage; so that of the varying penalties inflicted for similar crimes in different countries some must be unjustifiable. We have already seen that the utilitarian view has an equal difficulty in assessing the just penalty. It is important to notice that in few, if any, relations involving justice can desert be accurately determined. It will be agreed that we owe something in the way of deference to our parents, but he would be a bold man who should put forward any general limits either of age or extent. In legal contracts, indeed, there is a fixed payment for a specified service, but only the *legal* obligation is fixed; and for one party at least there is always an indeterminate margin between honest work or full measure on the one hand and the minimum that will pass inspection on the other. Moreover the scrupulous keeping of contracts would only correspond with the adherence to penalties legally proclaimed. The question corresponding to that of what penalties the law *should* proclaim is: What payment ought we to contract to give? The labourer is worthy

of some hire, but the difficulty of discovering an absolute exchange value for commodities or for labour has led us on utilitarian grounds to abide mainly by the higgling of the market. So, too, if a criminal have deserved to be treated as a means to the welfare of others, because he has treated others merely as a means to his own, we may within certain vague limits fix his punishment at what seems best calculated to secure the good of others and his own.

There are, in fact, no natural punishments indefeasible and universal any more than natural rights. For every man there is his due, for the evil and the good alike. Bad acts alter the situation and we cannot act as if they had been good. To say that guilt deserves its appropriate pain, if possible the pain of remorse, but if not, at least the communication of disapproval and alienation, is only to say that it is guilt. But disapproval may sometimes be communicated most effectively by coals of fire, sometimes by mere 'disgrace', sometimes by outlawry and treatment as a dangerous beast. *Δράσαντι παθεῖν.*

XIII
MORAL RULES

(90) ARE there, then, no valid moral rules? It will be agreed on all hands that no number of moral rules will save us from exercising intuition; for a rule can only be general, but an act must be particular, so it will always be necessary to satisfy ourselves that an act comes under the rule, and for this no rule can be given.

First we may notice that if there be such rules they may conflict. So having intuitively apprehended that, of two alternative acts possible for me, one is an instance of promise-keeping and the other an instance of saving innocent life, I should have intuitively to decide which is now 'my paramount duty', or, as I prefer to say, 'my duty' or 'my actual duty'. Those who speak of 'conflicting duties' seem to mean alternative possible acts, either of which, with very slight change of circumstance, would now be my plain duty, but between which I may well hesitate as to where that duty lies. If they conflict, only one is possible, so I cannot think that both can be my duty; nor should I blame myself for omitting the other. Rules get a specious universality by using dyslogistic terms. 'Thou shalt do no murder' meant 'Do no killing except justifiable homicide—such as stoning the blasphemer or wiping out the heathen.'

But, however they would need to be supplemented by intuition, such rules might be held to have a kind of provisional validity; so we must ask how they are ascertained. Probably all would agree that they are first seen and most clearly seen in individual instances.

I may repeat the decalogue, like the multiplication table, by rote, but when any doubt arises as to the universal validity of a precept I must follow the Socratic method and imagine, as definitely as may be, *instances* where my moral judgement would work. But if we can judge an instance without general rules, it might seem, as Butler says, that the inquiry after them is merely an occupation, not without some usefulness, for 'men of leisure'.[1] The usefulness suggested is, I suppose, that where the right course is obscure or the passions violent, rules may save the ship. So far as this is so I think that their function is that of ballast rather than compass. If the difficulty of acting rightly come from the difficulty of knowing what we now ought to do, whether that difficulty depend upon a real complexity of the situation or upon our own bias in the way of desire or prejudice, then we shall question any constraining rule and must, as a last resort, fix our attention upon the particular instance, in which, as is admitted, the validity of rules first and most clearly appears. And we shall be right. For since the rules are abstracted from instances and have to be applied to instances, to assume that this rule has been correctly formulated and applies to our present instance is to beg the question. The man who acts on principle is apt to be favourably contrasted with the man of 'impulse'; but principles may be wrong and *intuitions* right. We do not hear that Kant ever sacrificed an innocent life by telling the truth, but there is a tale of his condemning the conduct of some sailors who had thrown overboard in a dangerous storm a case of delicacies consigned to him. If the story be true it might be an instance when the idolatry of rules ('never

[1] Sermon III.

break a promise, even to save life') has worked *on the side of passion* against genuine moral insight. I think it probable that a pedantic desire for consistency with the hedonistic generalization which they thought self-evident has led some men to act wrongly, who would have acted rightly if they had no theory to justify. It has certainly led to the formulation of some very odd maxims. I cannot persuade myself that I first morally apprehend the obligation of several rules, then intellectually apprehend one of alternative actions to be an instance of one and the other of another, and finally, by a second moral intuition, see which rule ought now to be followed. I rather think that I morally apprehend that I ought now to do this act and then intellectually generalize rules.

(91) The real value of Kant's principle of universality is practical, not theoretical; it is a dodge, like asking an angry child to look at its face in a mirror. What is right for me to do in a particular instance is right, not because it would be right for others, but because the situation demands it from me or any one (if any one else could be in this situation), and I may judge more clearly if I imagine the agent to be some *one* else. By 'universalizing' my act I see it writ large. To analyse the situation and say that it is the factor A in it which morally demands the action B, and that therefore whenever A is present we ought to do B, is as hazardous as to analyse a work of art and produce those rules and canons of artistic production which pave the road to oblivion. There will always be other factors besides A, and their relevance must be seen, not proved. Perhaps this dispute is only verbal or I have misunderstood the position I am criticizing. Since, as I maintain, it is the situation

which determines what I now ought to do, if the character of that situation could be exhaustively described a rule for precisely similar situations could be given. This, of course, is impossible. But, it may be urged, we could thus give a rule for any situation which should differ in no *relevant* fact. I only contend that, for the reasons given, no such rules settle in advance how I ought now to act, and that the preoccupation with such generalities is on the whole apt to mislead us in deciding what is right, just as preoccupation with so-called canons of art is apt to mislead the artist.

But if the formulation of rules does not help us to decide what is now right, may it not help us on the whole to do right in general?—to steady, if not steer the ship? The use of rules may be defended as a very good practical dodge. If I cannot trust myself to choose rightly in the moment of temptation, is it not well to choose in a cool hour beforehand? Even granting that the decision may not always fit the situation when it comes, and that then, in abiding by my rule, I shall err, such errors will be less frequent, probably, than those I should have run into by trying to decide only when all the circumstances were before me, but consequently only when my passions were awake. If I keep a rule always to go to bed at a certain hour, that may on occasions be earlier or later than the circumstances really warrant, but it might on most days prevent me going much too late or too early out of slackness. I cannot imagine a man making rules for his conduct in cases where his passions would not be engaged; for instance, when his conduct would consist in exercising an immediate and unquestioned and disinterested control over the behaviour of another, and when it was not important for that other to know beforehand what would be enjoined. A man may usefully make rules for his own diet and hours of rest. But I suppose that no doctor would determine in advance how much food or sleep or work should be allowed to a given patient through his convalescence. All depends on the case.

(92) This use of rules for my own conduct is just analogous to justice and promise-keeping, as explained by Hume,[1] except that here the question need not be complicated by the expectations of other people. For, when other people depend upon my punctuality, it is not to keep a rule as such but to avoid wasting their time that is right. Hume saw that the individual act of justice may not produce so much pleasure as its omission, but argued that since justice *generally* does so, we should always do just acts.

The weakness of the dodge is that so soon as I recognize that there is no obligation to keep my own rules as such (if others do not rely on my doing so), but only when they really enjoin what I can see is right in this situation, then the fact that I have adopted a rule will leave my choice just as likely to be swayed by desire as if I had not adopted it. I shall be tempted to question the applicability of the rule, at least until I have formed a habit.

This is merely a case of the more general problem as to the nature and value of good resolutions. Really to will is to act. When I do what is called 'deciding' or 'making up my mind' beforehand, we know well enough that the 'decision' will often be abandoned; sometimes it should be. For, in deciding beforehand, not all the

[1] *Treatise of Human Nature*, III. ii. I only here reproduce so much of his view as suits my context.

circumstances can be known. And when the time for action comes, not only have I to decide whether the decision that I have made applies to this situation, but actually to decide over again; for, after all, I may have changed my mind. Yet, however irrational it may seem, good resolutions are made; and however inexplicable it be, they have some value. They help us to act rightly and so ought to be made. It is something, if not much, to 'decide' to get up early to-morrow or even always. So far then as we find rules necessary and useful we shall do well to make them; none of them are without exception, not even the rule not to act on rule; they are not quite rational, but neither are we. They may be *νοῦς ἄνευ ὀρέξεως*,[1] but also they are *νοῦς ἄνευ φρονήσεως*.

[1] Aristotle, *Politics* III. xvi.

XIV

THE MORAL FACULTY AND THE MORAL MOTIVE

(93) The question as to the nature of the moral faculty may be discussed very unprofitably and may conceal very improper assumptions. Butler,[1] probably following Aristotle,[2] allows rather contemptuously that the capacity by which 'we naturally and unavoidably approve some actions, under the peculiar view of their being virtuous and of good desert', may be 'considered as a sentiment of the understanding, or as a perception of the heart, or, which seems the truth, as including both'. He is clear enough, however, that its deliverances lay claim to truth and authority, and that these vital points are by implication obscured when it is spoken of as a moral *sense*.

It has long been recognized that we do not apprehend distinct faculties as we apprehend bodily organs,[3] but only infer them in order to account for our activities. But those who emphasize this truth have sometimes imitated their opponents by suggesting that to every class of 'object' there corresponds a single 'faculty' in the subject; as if we could never perceive the 'object' we had imagined nor remember what we had perceived.[4]

The better way of stating our ground for distinguishing faculties is that in our activities we immediately

[1] *Dissertation on Virtue.*

[2] *Ethics*, VI. ii. 5.

[3] Locke, *Essay on the Human Understanding*, II. xxi. 17; Sidgwick, *Methods of Ethics*, second edition, Bk. I, ch. iii.

[4] Cf. Plato, *Republic*, 477.

recognize resemblances and differences, as it were of flavour.[1]

(94) So the question we have to ask ourselves is this: Has the activity which we express by saying that an act is right more resemblance to that which we express by saying that we want to do it (or like doing it), or to that which we express by saying that (*a*) it will have beneficial consequences or (*b*) that once done it cannot be undone? The two last expressions, (*a*) and (*b*), would generally be said to depend upon an activity of reason; whereas wanting and liking would be ascribed to the 'faculty of desire' or of feeling. Yet since both the act which we want to do and the act which we ought to do are future, there has been a tendency to assume that one 'faculty' commends both; that our attitude to both is really the same. But this, as we have seen, is too hasty. There may be several activities related in a positive or affirmative way to future acts. For choosing or willing also bears some relation to the future, yet must be distinguished as a third activity and ascribed to a third 'faculty', since we do not always do either everything that we desire or everything that seems right.

So far I have laboured to avoid phrases such as *judging* or *thinking* or *knowing* an act to be right, since it might be said that, however natural, they really presuppose a theory which begs the question. But it is in fact inevitable to describe the experience in some such way. It is true that we also speak of *feeling that* an act is right. But when the word *feel* is followed by a clause of indirect statement, it is a colloquial equivalent of *think* or *believe*. I may say that I feel I am going to be ill or I feel I have been here before; but, though my

[1] Plato, *Republic*, 440.

feelings cannot be false, the judgement founded on them may. If we can be wrong about what is right it seems necessary to say that what was wrong was a judgement, that we *thought* falsely. We are apt to use the colloquialism 'feel that' when the judgement expressed in the indirect statement is the result of immediate apprehension and not of demonstration, and especially if it be a particular rather than a universal judgement. The judgement that this act is right is both indemonstrable and particular. Yet it is more like an apprehension of self-evident truth than it is like a perception of physical fact, since, though we can give no reason for it, we see its reasonableness. I feel that this act is agreeable, but I understand that it is wrong.

(95) It might still be held that, though to judge an act right is not equivalent to desiring to do it, it is equivalent to judging that I shall be pained at not having done it or that upon the whole I shall gain most satisfaction by doing it. This would involve identifying morality with prudence, on no better ground than that both differ from simple desire by implying reflection. As Kant saw, this deprives the words right and wrong of all meaning, since it denies that reason can discover distinctions of obligation between actions and reduces it to be the minister of desires which may differ in different persons. In Hume's language it implies that 'reason is, and ought only to be, the slave of the passions'.[1] But we are more clearly conscious of a difference between thinking an act prudent and thinking it right than we are of one between thinking it prudent and desiring to do it. Butler thought that, through God's justice, morality is always as a fact prudent; but

[1] *Treatise of Human Nature*, II. iii. 3.

he admitted that men cannot always see it to be so, and that his only reason for judging that it was so was because it *ought* to be. That is to say, it is only acts done solely because they are thought right, and not out of prudence, which deserve reward.

However little we care then for the antithesis, we must say that, as against Aristotle and the moral-sense school, Kant, and less emphatically Butler and the English rationalists, were right in assigning the awareness of a duty to a rational faculty.

(96) But thinking that I ought to do something is not the same as doing it, nor does it always lead to doing it. Will or choice is necessary. Can we then, without desire, will or choose to do what seems right, or must a desire to do it because we believe it right intervene? To accept the latter alternative would imply that we always do what we desire most and have in fact no choice or will. For if we could choose between a faint desire to do right and a stronger to do something else, when we chose to do right it would not be because we desired it. The suggestion that we *ought* most to desire to do what is right only puts the difficulty a stage further back. For, if we always must do what we most desire to do, we could only take steps to make ourselves most desire to do what is right if we most desired to take them. Whether we more desired to do our duty or something else would on this view depend upon our already determined character, and we should be left with no freedom of choice and no justification for remorse or censure. Yet we do feel satisfaction in *having* once done what we thought right and remorse for *having* done what we thought wrong, even if we now judge that this thinking was erroneous; though no satisfaction

in *having* satisfied a past desire or dissatisfaction in failure to have done so. Again, suppose it true that moral approval is simply our feeling towards a man who happens to desire to do what is right, because it is right, more than anything else. Then if, as a man grows older, his other desires naturally weaken and his desire to do what is right as such remain constant, he would more often deserve our moral admiration. But we do not think this.

It seems to me that when we do an act which we think right we are often conscious of a much greater desire to do something else. And this implies that we can choose to do an act on some other ground than the desire to do it, even the desire to do it because it is right. And the only evidence for our having a desire is that we feel it, and for a desire being stronger that we feel it to be stronger. To assume that we must have acted from the strongest desire is to beg the question. So far as prima facie probabilities go, I should expect that a rational being who is also a practical and desiring being, if it be granted that he can see a way of acting to be right, could make that perceived rightness the ground of his choice; but not that he must.

XV

FREEDOM

(97) It is clear that we have at last been driven into considering the question of freedom. The implied reluctance to raise it arises not merely from its difficulty, but from the feeling that our chance of answering it, even more than any other moral question, depends upon our having cleared our minds upon other moral questions first. For I believe that Kant was right in saying that, though freedom is the *ratio essendi* or condition of morality, morality is the *ratio cognoscendi* or evidence of freedom. The best way of approaching the question is to begin by asking what we mean by human freedom, or better still what we mean by an action as distinct from an event. An involuntary action is a contradiction in terms. For when I am dragged or pushed by others the action is theirs, and when my heart beats or my memory fails that is an event. From these involuntary affections of my mind and body most people distinguish what they would call voluntary acts or acts of choice, and also perhaps an intermediate or uncertain class of extreme mental dispositions, when they would say that, owing to pain or excitement or exhaustion or terror, I was 'hardly responsible' for my acts, 'scarcely my own master'.

It seems to be only an undue preoccupation with the methods of the physical sciences which has sometimes led people to forget or to deny this distinction. They have conceived the material world as a closed system whose condition at any moment is necessarily determined solely by its preceding condition. To suggest, then, that the present distribution of matter, for instance the pattern of printer's ink on this page, is in any degree due to thoughts, desires, or any of those non-spatial concomitants of bodily movement which have undoubtedly occurred in me while I read and wrote, or in the printers while they set it up, would be absurd. Consciousness is thus reduced to an irrelevant by-product or *epiphenomenon*, accompanying the bodily movements which are completely determined by the movements of other bodies, but in no way modifying them. Such a view, though paradoxical, is surely unscientific. If, as seems to be allowed, the mental facts be caused by physical facts, it is merely dogmatic to assert that they cannot react upon matter. Or if the two worlds be wholly unrelated, and my ideas be in no way causally conditioned by physical happenings, there seems little reason to suppose that I know anything about the physical world or that it exists.

(98) To admit that mental events may be links in the necessary chain of causality is, however, by no means to admit freedom or even, I think, to distinguish an act from an event. We should not call a quickened pulse an act, though we think that it would not have quickened if the man had not *understood* the words he heard.

The mechanistic view of action, which really regards us as automata, being abandoned, we might still hold that every act is absolutely determined by the character of the self, with its desires, as acted upon by the environment at any moment; and those who take this to be the fact are apt to call it freedom, on the ground that what determines our act is nothing but our own character. Much may be said for this view, but it is worth noticing that any prejudice in its favour due to an analogy with the physical world seems ill-founded. Once granted that changes in the material world can have causes other than physical, can for instance be caused by a desire that they should take place, we have manifestly passed out of the world where the 'uniformity of nature' as understood by the physicist holds good, and our question must be decided on the introspective or the critical method more proper to philosophy. I do not think that physical causation is strictly any more *intelligible* than psychological causation; nor psychological than freedom.

(99) Kant puts the position clearly: 'If I say of a man who commits a theft that, by the physical law of causality, this deed is a necessary result of the determining causes in preceding time . . . how can the judgement that it ought not to have been done make any difference? . . . Some try to evade this by saying that the causes which determine his action lie *within* him. . . . This would only be the sense in which we speak of *free* motion of a projectile, meaning that it is not urged on, deflected, or resisted by anything external. . . . This is a wretched subterfuge by which some still let themselves be put off, and so think that they have solved with a petty verbal juggling this eternal problem. If, as they admit, the ideas which determine the man have their ground of existence in time and in the antecedent state, it does not matter if these antecedent states are internal or external, and whether their causality is psychological or mechanical, i. e. whether they produce acts by means of ideas or of physical movements; they are still deter-

mining principles in a temporal sequence.'[1] This and several other passages in Kant lead us to expect from him a defence of free choice in the actions of moral beings. But in the end the 'wretched subterfuge' offered us is that all our acts are phenomenally determined by desires and therefore bad, all are noumenally determined by reason and therefore good. So the same acts are all good and all bad and none are free. He has deceived himself by the analogy of moral law to laws of nature which 'determine' the behaviour of all to which they apply. And I think that he also suffers from that idolatry of freedom which both in philosophy and in politics has led men to suppose that there cannot be a freedom to do wrong, that unless it turn out well liberty is 'merely licence'. Truly that literal 'slavery to the passions' which Kant attributes to beasts is below freedom, but that 'determination by reason' which he attributes to a 'holy will' is above it.[2] For the mixed

[1] *Critique of Practical Reason.* Abbott: *Kant's Ethics*, p. 189, summarized.

[2] Kant states his doctrine briefly and explicitly in the *Prolegomena to any Future Metaphysic* (§ 53). All acts are phenomenally determined; even moral acts are determined by the maxim followed (I suppose so far as desire to follow it is aroused). All acts are noumenally free; in moral acts reason is the cause of the natural law by which we follow our maxim, and reason acts from objective obligation which is no part of the time series (for the 'ought' is still unrealized); even in immoral acts the reason is not influenced by desire, so remains free. In his note to this section Kant admits that 'a purely intellectual being (*Verstandeswesen*), e.g. God, so far as his action is immanent, would not come under any concept of freedom. For his action, though not dependent on external determining causes, is yet determined in his eternal reason, that is, in his divine nature.' Only those acts

nature of mankind there may be a choice between satisfying desire and obeying reason. In any event the only freedom which interests the moral philosopher is the freedom of those acts which Kant would call phenomenal.

(100) We have already seen[1] that, if the determining motive of every act be desire, then the strongest desire must always be followed; for if a weaker desire were followed it could only be because of some other motive. But, if it be allowed that the recognition of the rightness of an action can be followed by the doing of that action, we still have two views to consider. One is that our character, being what it is owing to our original nature and our past history, determines us to desire most to do either what we think right or something else; and in either case to do what we most desire to do. The other is that our character determines indeed our desires and also what we think right, and consequently the alternative acts between which we have to choose, but must not be counted a second time as determining that choice.

The supporters of the first view maintain that acts are free if they spring of necessity from our own nature and character, that is to say, from our desires and from the beliefs which may have conditioned those desires. And further they affirm that their view allows both for the distinction of right and wrong and for the validity of remorse and of censure or punishment. It is on the

which originate something in the phenomenal world of time and sense (into which desire enters) involve freedom, which is the *power of spontaneously originating an event*. This note seems to imply a view like my own.

[1] See §§ 26 and 96.

last of these two points, namely on remorse and censure, that their case seems most vulnerable. If I be the kind of person who by the necessity of my nature do acts which I think wrong, I may well regret it and even be ashamed of it; as I may regret the bad memory which (through a necessity of my own mind) makes me a nuisance to myself and others, or as I may be ashamed of my personal appearance, my stupidity, or my insensitiveness to music. None of these shames are precisely similar, and yet, I think, all resemble one another in a degree in which they do not resemble remorse, whose specific character is to be regret or shame for that which I could have helped. Again, I may dislike or despise those who are feeble, ugly, stupid, vulgar, or forgetful. But I only censure them for that which I believe they could have helped. Punishment and reward presuppose guilt and desert. My own conclusion, then, would be that such 'self-determinism' would make merit and remorse depend upon illusion. If I be correct, we must then go on to ask whether it could even be consistent with the distinction of right and wrong. If I believed that men act as they do because their nature is what it is, I could doubtless distinguish useful from noxious actions, and also those whose contemplation gave me a quasi-aesthetic satisfaction from those which did not; but it is not clear to me that I could form the conception of right, that is, obligatory acts. To say that I ought to do what my nature either compels me to do or prevents me from doing is difficult, even if it be asserted that it would be just this alleged obligatory character that would appeal or not appeal to my nature. If it be true that I ought to do something, it must be true that my nature does not render me incapable of doing it. Before I could come to believe that I ought to do something I should have to believe that I was capable of doing it if I thought that I ought.

(101) To suppose then that, between alternatives which are absolutely determined, we exercise, whenever we recognize a duty, a choice which is absolutely spontaneous, seems to me the hypothesis best fitted to explain our moral experience. And it is no more opposed to science than is any theory which distinguishes *actions* from events. It is also the hypothesis most consonant with the evidence of introspection. On this, however, I lay less stress, as some people would assert that they seem to themselves to have the same freedom of choice between alternatives neither of which is recognized as obligatory. And in this it seems that they must be mistaken. If moral beings can ever 'act' without raising the question of duty, it would seem that they can only 'act' in accordance with their strongest desire, and the freedom that they then have is only that of self-determination: their acts spring inevitably from their natures. If I am asked whether I will take beef or mutton and if I know of no obligation to choose either, I must take that which, on whatever grounds, I desire to take most. If I have to pick up one of two indistinguishable and adjacent pins it would seem absurd to say that I am free to choose, for there is nothing to choose. I suppose that I must take the one which is easier to take—unless I desire to prove that I can take the one which is more difficult. This is the freedom of indifference ridiculed by determinists. And even introspection corroborates this distinction. In 'choosing' between two pins I am merely conscious of the absence of external compulsion; in choosing

between doing my duty and doing what I want I am conscious of struggle and effort.

It is sometimes objected that we claim to be determined, as when a man says, 'You might have known me better than to suspect me of such a meanness'. I think that such expressions only mean that to some people the idea of picking a friend's pocket simply does not appeal: they are not free to do such an act. I fancy that, without a severe training, considerably modifying my present character, I *could* not commit a very bloody murder. We certainly cannot do what we neither desire nor think right. Perhaps the converse is also true: we might say, 'You ought to have known me better than to submit me to such a temptation'. I think that I *could* not, without a great change of character, endure some kinds of martyrdom. So far as I thought it right I could at least try, and if under pain or fear I really 'lost control of myself' the responsibility would not be mine.

Determinists have also asserted that, if men were really free, it would be folly to think that we could affect their conduct by our words or deeds, and 'thus almost all the actions with which morality is concerned would become irrational, rational action would be wholly precluded from trying to influence people's volitions'.[1] If men be free to choose between alternatives, why on earth should we not try to alter the alternatives, or their view of the alternatives, between which they are free to choose? A man may have before him the alternatives of enjoying illicit gain or paying his debts. As magistrate I can substitute the alternatives of paying his debts or going to prison. If he be good this will not alter his

[1] Russell, *Philosophical Essays*, p. 39.

conduct, and I should not wish to do so; but if he be bad it probably will. Even as a preacher I may by eloquence arouse his pity and so make one alternative more attractive, or by pointing out obligations that he had failed to notice, I may actually introduce the alternative of duty when he had only seen various possibilities of profit.

(102) As students of moral philosophy we are not immediately concerned with theological problems. But we must notice that one motive for rejecting freedom has been the reluctance to suppose that human actions can escape divine fore-knowledge. It has often been pointed out in reply that to deny that God could create free beings is to limit his power in the interests of his knowledge. But I believe that what has really weighed with religious people has been less the conviction that God must know whether we shall try to do right than the conviction that he could not trust the destiny of the human race, even in this world, to an incalculable freedom. But we have admitted that the alternatives between which I choose are both determined, though no doubt partly determined by my past choices. And I may be quite wrong in my calculation of consequences. An act which I do, believing it to be wrong because I think that it sacrifices the community's health to mine, may do precisely the opposite. My guilt is undiminished, but so are the useful consequences. It is just conceivable, though almost infinitely improbable, that all acts done, even the most immoral, might be the most felicific possible or even actually right. Only on some such daring act of faith can I understand Hegel's gloss on Schiller's epigram, *Die Weltgeschichte ist das Weltgericht*, though he often seems to mean a judge-

ment on the *morality* of acts and the *merit* of agents, to which the subsequent history of the world could be no index.[1]

> ἄγου δέ μ', ὦ Ζεῦ, καὶ σύ γ' ἡ Πεπρωμένη,
> ὅποι ποθ' ὑμῖν εἰμι διατεταγμένος·
> ὡς ἕψομαί γ' ἄοκνος· ἢν δέ γε μὴ θέλω,
> κακὸς γενόμενος, οὐδὲν ἧττον ἕψομαι.[2]

(103) At any rate freedom of moral choice seems to me the only hypothesis which offers even a hint at a possible solution of the problem of evil. As Kant pointed out, were happiness the only good in the world we should have to confess the world very evil, for we are not provided with a very adequate instrument in reason for securing that good. But if the only thing unconditionally good is a good will, in the sense of a free choice of what is right as against what is desired, we should understand the presence of two kinds of evil in the world, if not the actual amount and distribution of them. The possibility of moral action implies the possibility of immoral action, that is, of moral evil; and the possibility of moral action implies the presence of pain and unsatisfied desires both in ourselves and others. For if others did not want anything we could have no duties to them; and if we ourselves did not want anything we could not be free, for our acts would be necessarily determined by reason. On the day on which evil were eliminated from the world morality and freedom would vanish with it. This, I suppose, is what Hegel[3]

[1] *Philosophie des Rechts*, III. iii. c. 340.

[2] Epictetus, *Encheiridion* 53 q. from Cleanthes.

[3] *Phänomenologie des Geistes*, V.C (AA) B. (c.) (Baillie translation, pp. 372–5) freely paraphrased. I suppose that the good always triumphs so far as men try to do what is right.

means when he says that morality knows in its heart that the good always triumphs, or is always triumphing, for the fight is a sham fight, in which morality[1] only engages to keep its weapons bright and the enemy's no less. The essential good of the world's process, which the good man proposes to establish as the *result* of his morality, is just his own moral action. The struggle is itself the end.

[1] Hegel speaks of *Tugend* in his usual depreciatory sense.

XVI

CONCLUSION

(104) For those who have persevered through the preceding chapters a summary of the positions to which I have from time to time committed myself may be useful. Those who have not done so could only find such a summary misleading. For if I had been able to state my views as convincingly and unambiguously in short as at length, I should not have done it at length.

I will begin by recapitulating my terminology. Here I should have liked to keep closer to recognized usage. But, after questioning a good many careful users of language, I concluded that those who had no philosophical doctrine to support were in no sort of agreement as to the precise meaning of words like 'moral' and 'virtuous'; while several kinds of act which need mention have no recognized names. I have therefore had to apply current words rather arbitrarily.

When we think a particular possible act to be right for us to do now, but desire not to do it more than to do it, or desire more to do something inconsistent with doing it, we can choose either course.

If we do what we think wrong or fail to do what we think right we act *immorally*, and the *guilt* is in proportion to our clear consciousness of stringency in the obligation. If we do the act that we think right, and do it for that reason simply, we act *morally*, and the *merit* is in proportion to the strength of the desires resisted. Moral and immoral acts are spontaneous acts of choice: they are free in the fullest sense.

If, however, we do the act that we think right simply

because we desire to do it (apart from thinking it right) more than we desire not to do it or to do anything inconsistent with doing it, I should not call the act moral. When the desire that we act upon is of a kind that usually leads to right acts, and therefore ought to be encouraged, I call it a *virtuous* act. When, on the other hand, the desire is of a kind that usually leads to wrong acts, and therefore ought to be discouraged, I call it, for lack of a proper name, a *vicious* act; though I doubt if many people would apply the term to an act which the agent thought right, however bad its motive. An example of such an act would be if I told the truth, believing that I now ought to tell it, yet not for that reason, but in order to give pain. Perhaps even an immoral act could sometimes be called virtuous; when, for instance, I do an act, which I recognize to be wrong, out of patriotism.

Again, if people do an act, thinking it right, because they desire to do right acts as such more than they desire not to do this act or than they desire to do anything inconsistent with doing it, such an act might be called *saintly*. In such people, reverence for the moral law has become a hunger and thirst after righteousness; and such acts are neither moral, virtuous, nor free, in the strict sense that I have given to those words. I can do an act which I think right, lastly, with no desires one way or the other; this apparently is what Kant calls a *holy* act and regards as characteristic of the divine will and our own noumenal wills; yet an instance would occur whenever a judge, who has absolutely no interest in either party, gives a just decision. All the acts so far described, except the immoral act, are thought right by the doer; but, so far as we have described them, all might be wrong. It is possible to suggest other kinds of act, besides the immoral act, which might be done by a man believing them to be wrong. The extreme antithesis to a holy act would be one done simply because it was believed wrong, without any desire; and as this is inconceivable I should simply call it *monstrous*. The correlative of a saintly act would be one done simply from the desire to do wrong as such; I do not think that this occurs outside melodrama, but it would be a *satanic* act. So perhaps the only acts ever done in the belief that they are wrong are immoral acts; and these may sometimes be right. Besides all these I think that there are *indifferent* 'acts': acts which we can recognize no obligation whatever either to do or to leave undone. The list, then, would be as follows:

I. Acts done in the belief that they are right:
  (1) Holy (= 4 but without adverse impulse or choice).
  (2) Saintly.
  (3) Virtuous.
  (4) *Moral.*
  (5) Vicious.

II. Acts done in the belief that they are wrong:
  (6) *Immoral.* (Some of these might be called virtuous and some vicious.)
  (7) Satanic.
  (8) Monstrous.

III. Indifferent acts.

(105) I think that the recognition of the difference between right and wrong is properly called rational, and that the distinction is first made in particular situations where a definite possible act is thought of as obligatory. But the rightness of an act cannot be deduced from the notion of rightness nor inferred from

any goodness in the result which it will bring about. Nor do I think that there are any rules for conduct which we know always ought to be followed: we must always consider the whole situation in which we have to act and the ways in which our action may affect it; and consequently there is nothing to which anybody under all possible circumstances has a right. But whatever we ought to do for anybody he has a right that we should do (cf. §§ 79 and 82).

Yet, though the rightness of an act does not depend upon the amount of satisfaction which it will produce, every right act does produce some satisfaction for somebody, namely that which is due to him, and perhaps always some for the doer, apart from the satisfaction taken in the performance of a moral act. If the last suggestion be true, it would follow that only acts in which we have some interest, generally through sympathy, occur to us, and consequently only these are thought right for ourselves to do, though other possible acts can of course be right. If that were so conscience would be purely critical.

We say truly enough in general terms that guilt deserves punishment and merit deserves reward, but we cannot say in general how much of either, and both should sometimes be remitted.

I do not think that it can be our duty to act from a good desire, since desires are not directly in our power, but only to do what we believe really right. Among the desires we have, we could only judge which it is now right to follow by considering whether the act it prompts us to is right.

Consistently, I hope, with the views just enumerated, I do not think that right conduct can properly be defined as following the highest motive, or willing coherently, or as realizing or sacrificing the self; nor yet as promoting morality, or the common good, or the evolution of the species, or the greatest happiness of the greatest number or of the doer. And I think that those who assert that we always follow the strongest desire or the desire for our own greatest pleasure are mistaken.

I have not satisfied myself that there is any quality common to all right acts which makes them right. I think that probably most right acts consist in bringing about the distribution of satisfactions which is due in the circumstances. But I attach little importance to this phrase for two reasons. The first is that 'due' is only a synonym for 'right'. The other is that a man may have a duty, where other people are not concerned, to make the best use of his faculties; and, though this will give him some satisfaction, it seems improper to distinguish it from the satisfaction which he might have got out of sloth or appetite as being a satisfaction due from himself to himself.

To me the most puzzling point in ethics is that though we cannot suppose a man's duties to depend on his recognizing them, yet (1) he would not have any duties unless he were a rational being capable of recognizing them, and (2) since he can have no duties which he cannot perform, it seems as if unavoidable ignorance should modify his duties as much as physical weakness. Most systems of ethics, as I understand them, have conspicuously failed to help us in this difficulty. I think we must say that there are right acts for a rational being to perform, whether he knows what they all are or not, but that we cannot blame him for not doing them if he cannot know them.

Of ethical writers I think that Kant and Butler come nearest to the truth, though I have also learned much, among the moderns, from Lotze and Martineau. But my opinions upon these matters have suffered a pretty constant development, and I have no reason to fear that this has ceased even if *vires demittit eundo*.

BIBLIOGRAPHY

I. INTRODUCTORY BOOKS.

L. DICKINSON: *The Meaning of Good.* London.

An attractive and stimulating dialogue in which the parties put forward and discuss conversationally various theories of the end of life.

G. E. MOORE: *Ethics* (Home University Library). London, and Holt & Co., New York.

A short book which, in a very careful discussion of two or three ethical questions—does the rightness of an act depend upon its being thought right, or upon its consequences, or upon neither? what is meant by freedom?—gives an example of the accuracy of statement necessary for philosophical discussion. The author decides that the rightness of an act depends upon its consequences.

B. RUSSELL: *Philosophical Essays.* I. *The Elements of Ethics.* London.

The main view is similar to that of Mr. Moore's book, but more questions are touched and the manner is lighter and more stimulating.

G. C. FIELD: *Introduction to Ethical Theory.* London, and Dutton, New York.

A comparison of theories, exemplified by Aristotle, which put the rightness of action in its subservience to a state of happiness or self-realization (identified by the author with love), with theories, exemplified by Kant, which put it in obedience to reason. The author discusses both sympathetically and decides for the former.

J. S. MILL: *Utilitarianism.*

A short pamphlet defending the view which founds utilitarianism on the hedonistic psychology.

II. STANDARD MODERN WORKS.

H. RASHDALL: *The Theory of Good and Evil.* Oxford.

The most recent work adequately covering the whole field of moral philosophy, in two volumes. The author's own point of view may be described as a modification of rational or altruistic utilitarianism. He believes that all right action is directed to the production of some 'good', rationally recognized as such, and that one such good is pleasure. Moral action is, however, itself a good of the highest value. These positions are argued at length and criticism of them considered. The metaphysic implied is 'personal idealism'.

H. Sidgwick: *Methods of Ethics.* Macmillan.

The best exposition of the rationalist or altruistic utilitarian theory.

T. H. Green: *Prolegomena to Ethics.* Oxford.

An exposition of the view that right action is that which contributes to the common good, with criticism of other theories. Book I is a somewhat obscure idealist metaphysic which the student may omit on first reading. Book II deals with the will.

H. Sidgwick: *History of Ethics.* Macmillan.

J. Martineau: *Types of Ethical Theory.* Oxford.

A survey of the chief types of ethical theory arranged as I. Unpsychological, A. Metaphysical, i. Transcendental, e.g. Plato; ii. Immanental, e.g. Descartes, Malebranche, Spinoza. B. Physical, e.g. Comte. II. Psychological. A. Idiopsychological, e.g. Martineau. B. Heteropsychological, i. Hedonist, e.g. Hobbes, Mill, Bentham, Bain; ii. Rationalist, e.g. Cudworth, Clarke; iii. Aesthetic, e.g. Shaftesbury, Hutcheson. Martineau's own view is that we have no means of judging an action absolutely right, but on any given occasion of action we find in ourselves several impulses or springs of action, which we must value in a gradation of worth. We are absolutely free to choose which of these impulses we shall carry out, and the choice of what is judged the highest among those present is the moral act. The function of reason is to determine how the selected impulse may be most efficiently carried out.

F. H. Bradley: *Ethical Studies.* Oxford.

Separate essays written from a Hegelian point of view on such subjects as Pleasure, Self-realization, My Station and its Duties, Freedom, Duty for Duty's Sake. The manner is uncompromisingly brilliant and stimulating.

G. E. Moore: *Principia Ethica*. Cambridge.

An acute criticism of many ethical fallacies. The author's own realistic view of rightness is developed with great dialectical skill and fearless disregard of paradoxical consequences.

B. Croce: *Filosofia della Pratica*. Bari. (*Philosophy of the Practical*, translated by D. Ainslie.)

J. Grote: *A Treatise on the Moral Ideals*. Cambridge.

Papers posthumously collected and, partly for that reason, rather desultory. Though the manner is dry, the analysis of fundamental moral ideas is admirably searching.

III. THE CLASSICAL AUTHORITIES.

Plato, especially *The Republic* (several translations); also *Protagoras*, *Gorgias*, *Philebus* (translated by Jowett).

Aristotle: *The Nicomachean Ethics* (translated by W. D. Ross).

Hobbes: *Leviathan* (Parts I and II).

Butler: *Dissertation of the Nature of Virtue*. *Sermons* (especially Preface).

Hume: *Treatise of Human Nature*, Books II and III. *Enquiry concerning the Principles of Morals*.

Kant: *Foundation of Metaphysic of Morals*. *Critique of Practical Reason* (translated by Abbott in *Kant's Theory of Ethics*).

PRINTED IN GREAT BRITAIN AT THE UNIVERSITY PRESS, OXFORD
BY JOHN JOHNSON, PRINTER TO THE UNIVERSITY